SWAMI VIVEKANANDA

ON

INDIA AND HER PROBLEMS

SWAMI VIVEKANANDA

ON

INDIA AND HER PROBLEMS

COMPILED BY

SWAMI NIRVEDANANDA

GYAN

Published by

Gyan Publishing House
5, Ansari Road
Daryaganj, New Delhi-110002
Phone: 011-47034999, 9811692060
E-mail: books@gyanbooks.com

Distribution Network
gyanbooks.com
India, USA, Canada, UK, Australia

ISBN: 978-93-6780-645-6 (HB)

First Published, 1910

2nd Impression 2024

Printed at: Gyan Press, Delhi.

SWAMI VIVEKANANDA ON INDIA AND HER PROBLEMS
Compiler: SWAMI NIRVEDANANDA

SWAMI VIVEKANANDA
ON
INDIA AND HER PROBLEMS

SWAMI VIVEKANANDA

ON

INDIA AND HER PROBLEMS

COMPILED BY
SWAMI NIRVEDANANDA

ADVAITA ASHRAMA
MAYAVATI, ALMORA, HIMALAYAS.

CONTENTS

CHAPTER V: UPLIFT OF THE MASSES

CHAPTER VI: CASTE PROBLEM

CHAPTER VII: UPLIFT OF WOMEN

CHAPTER VIII: INVIGORATING CULTURAL LIFE

FOREWORD

"I have a message for the world, which I will deliver without fear and care for the future. To the reformers I will point out that I am a greater reformer than any one of them. They want to reform only little bits, I want root-and-branch reform."

—*Swami Vivekananda*

It is an irony of fate that posterity defies the Cross on which contemporaries feel no scruple to nail a prophet. A prophet's message is always based on a clear, deep and far-reaching vision of things, which are much beyond the ken of his contemporaries. This is why humanity is always late in accepting him.

Swami Vivekananda, the illustrious apostle of Sri Ramakrishna, was endowed with a prophet's vision. He has delivered unto the world his message, and it behoves us that we become wiser by history and lose no time in making an earnest effort to understand, appreciate and carry out his message.

His message is not for the hour, but for the age, not for the nation only, but for humanity. So far as India is concerned, his message is not meant for little bits of social or religious reform, but for a complete rejuvenation of her national life in all its phases.

The following pages contain a few extracts from his speeches and writings bearing on various Indian problems. The gleanings have been made from *The Complete*

Works of Swami Vivekananda published by the Advaita Ashrama, Mayavati and arranged to form a number of topics regarding India and her problems.

THE
RAMAKRISHNA MISSION
STUDENTS' HOME
Calcutta 1925

COMPILER

PREFACE TO THE FOURTH EDITION

The fourth edition presents the book in an altogether new form. The different topics concerning India and her problems have been thoroughly revised, rearranged and, in most cases, renamed. Moreover, the extracts culled from different portions of *The Complete Works* of Swami Vivekananda have been so arranged as to make continuous articles under different topical heads.

The book in its present form is expected to prove more useful and interesting than the previous editions. Our labour will be amply rewarded if it goes to enlighten and inspire all who have the well-being of India at heart.

July, 1946

COMPILER

CHAPTER I

OUR MOTHERLAND

Her Eminence

If there is any land on this earth that can lay claim to be the blessed *punya bhumi* (holy land), to be the land to which all souls on this earth must come to account for *karma*, the land to which every soul that is wending its way Godward must come to attain its last home, the land where humanity has attained its highest towards gentleness, towards generosity, towards purity, towards calmness, above all, the land of introspection and of spirituality—it is India. This is the ancient land where wisdom made its home before it went into any other country, the same India whose influx of spirituality is represented, as it were, on the material plane, by rolling rivers like oceans, where the eternal Himalayas, rising tier above tier with their snow-caps, look as it were into the very mysteries of heaven. Here is the same India whose soil has been trodden by the feet of the greatest sages that ever lived. Here first sprang up inquiries into the nature of man, and into the internal world. Here first arose the doctrines of the immortality of the soul, the existence of a supervising God, an immanent God in Nature and in man, and here the highest ideals of religion and philosophy have attained their culminating points.

Our sacred motherland is a land of religion and philosophy—the birthplace of spiritual giants—the land of renunciation, where and where alone, from the most ancient to the most modern times, there has been the highest ideal of life open to man. This is the motherland of philosophy, of spirituality, and of ethics, of sweetness, gentleness, and love. These still exist, and my experience of the world leads me to stand on firm ground, and make the bold statement, that India is still the first and foremost of all the nations of the world in these respects.

It is the same India which has withstood the shocks of centuries, of hundreds of foreign invasions, hundreds of upheavals of manners and customs. It is the same land which stands firmer than any rock in the world, with its undying vigour, indestructible life. Its life is of the same nature as the Soul, without beginning and without end, immortal, and we are the children of such a country. Here activity prevailed when even Greece did not exist, when Rome was not thought of, when the very fathers of the modern Europeans lived in the forests and painted themselves blue. Even earlier, when history has no record, and tradition dares not peer into the gloom of that intense past, even from then until now, ideas after ideas have marched out from her, but every word has been spoken with a blessing behind it and peace before it. Study the history of the whole world, and you will see that every high ideal you meet with anywhere had its origin in India. From time immemorial India has been the mine of precious ideas to human society: giving birth to high ideas herself, she has freely distributed them broadcast over the whole world. Religious researches disclose to us the fact, that there is not a country possessing a good ethical code but has borrowed something of it from us, and there is not one religion possessing good ideas of immortality of the soul but has derived it directly or indirectly from us. This is the land from whence, like the tidal waves, spirituality and philosophy have again and again rushed out and deluged the world, and this is the land from whence once more such tides must proceed in order to bring life and vigour into the decaying races of mankind.

The debt which the world owes to our motherland is immense. Taking country with country, there is not one race on this earth to which the world owes so much as to the patient Hindu, the mild Hindu. Like the gentle dew that falls unseen and unheard, and yet brings into blossom the fairest of roses, has been the contribution of India to the thought of the world. Silent, unperceived, yet omnipotent in its effect, it has revolutionized the thought of the world, yet nobody knows when it did so.

In ancient times and in modern times, great ideas have emanated from strong and great races. In ancient and modern times, wonderful ideas have been carried forward from one race to another. In ancient and modern times, seeds of great truth and power have been cast abroad by the advancing tides of national life, but mark you, it has been always with the blast of war trumpets, and with the march of embattled cohorts. Each idea had to be soaked in a deluge of blood; each idea had to wade through the blood of millions of our fellow-beings; each word of power had to be followed by the groans of millions, by the wails of orphans, by the tears of widows. This, in the main, other nations have taught; but India has for thousands of years peacefully existed.

They (the Western people) talk a great deal of the new theories about the survival of the fittest, and they think that it is the strength of the muscles which is the fittest to survive. If that were true, any one of the aggressively known old world nations would have lived in glory today, and we, the weak Hindus, who never conquered even one other race or nation ought to have died out, yet we live here three hundred millions strong! We, of all nations of the world, have never been a conquering race, and that blessing is on our head, and therefore we live.

Vanished from off the face of the earth, with not even a tale left behind to tell, gone is that ancient land of the Greeks. There was a time when the Roman Eagle floated over everything worth having in this world; everywhere Rome's power was felt and pressed on the head of humanity; the earth trembled at the name of Rome. But the Capitoline Hill is a mass of ruins, the spider weaves its web where the Caesars ruled. There have been other nations equally glorious that have come and gone, living a few hours of exultant and of exuberant dominance, and of a wicked national life, and then vanishing like ripples on the face of the waters. Thus have these nations made their mark on the face of humanity. But we live; and if Manu came back today he would not be bewildered, and would not find himself in a foreign land. The same laws are here, laws adjusted and tho ght out through thousands and thousands of years; customs, the outcome of the acumen of ages and the experience of centuries, that seem to be eternal; and as the days go by, as blow after blow of misfortune has been delivered upon them, they seem to have served one purpose only, that of making them stronger and more constant.

Did you ever hear of a country, where the greatest kings tried to trace their descent, not to kings, not to robber-barons living in old castles, who plundered poor travellers, but to semi-naked sages who lived in the forest? . . . This is the land. I am one of the proudest men ever born, but let me tell you frankly, it is not for myself, but on account of my ancestry. The more I have studied the past, the more I have looked back, more and more has this pride come to me, and it has given me the strength and courage of conviction, raised me up from the dust of the earth, and set me working out that great plan laid out by those great ancestors of ours. Children of those ancient Aryans, through the grace of the Lord may you have the same pride, may that faith in your ancestors come into your blood, may it become a part and parcel of your lives, may it work towards the salvation of the world! Here is the life-giving water with which must be quenched the burning fire of materialism which is burning the core of the hearts of millions, in other lands.

Her Life Centre

Each nation has its own part to play, and naturally, each nation has its own peculiarity and individuality' with which it is born. Each represents, as it were, one peculiar note in this harmony of nations, and this is its very life, its vitality. In it is the backbone, the foundation, and the bed-rock of the national life. In one nation political power is its vitality, as in England. Artistic life in another, and so on. I have seen that I cannot preach even religion to Americans without showing them its practical effect on social life. I could not preach religion in England without showing the wonderful political changes the Vedanta would bring.

Here in this blessed land, the foundation, the backbone, the life-centre is religion and religion alone. In India, religious life forms the centre, the keynote of the whole music of national life. Let others talk of politics, of the glory of acquisition of immense wealth poured in by trade, of the power and spread of commercialism, of the glorious fountain of physical liberty, but these the Hindu mind does not understand and does not want to understand. Touch him on spirituality, on religion, on God, on the soul, on the Infinite, on spiritual freedom, and I assure you, the lowest peasant in India is better informed on these subjects than many a so-called philosopher in other lands.

So, in India, social reform has to be preached by showing how much more spiritual a life the new system will bring; and politics has to be preached by showing how much it will improve the one thing that the nation wants—its spirituality. Every man has to make his own choice; so has every nation.

We made our choice ages ago and we must abide by it. And, after all, it is not such a bad choice. Is it such a bad choice in this world to think, not of matter but of spirit, not of man but of God? That intense faith in another world, that intense hatred for this world, that intense power of renunciation, that intense faith in God, that intense faith in the immortal soul, is in you. I challenge anyone to give it up. You cannot. You may try to impose upon me by becoming materialists, by talking materialism for a few months, but I know what you are; if I take you by the hand, back you come as good theists as ever were born. How can you change your nature? Your talks of politics, of social regeneration, your talks of money-making, and commercialism—all these will roll off like water from a duck's back.

For good or for evil, our vitality is concentrated in our religion. You cannot change it. You cannot destroy it and put in its place another. You cannot transplant a large growing tree from one soil to another and make it immediately take root there. For good or for evil, the religious ideal has been flowing into India for thousands of years; for good or for evil, the Indian atmosphere has been filled with ideals of religion for shining scores of centuries; for good or for evil, we have been born and brought up in the very midst of these ideals of religion, till it has entered into our very blood, and tingled with every drop in our veins, and has become one with our constitution, become the very vitality of our lives. Can you give such religion up without the rousing of the same energy in reaction, without filling the channel which that mighty river has cut out for itself in the course of thousands of years? Do you want that the Ganges should go back to its icy bed and begin a new course? Even if that were possible, it would be impossible for this country to give up her characteristic courage of religious life and take up for herself a new career of politics or something else. You can only work under the law of least resistance, and this religious line is the line of least resistance in India. This is the line of life, this is the line of growth, and this is the line of well-being in India—to follow the track of religion.

If any nation attempts to throw off its national vitality, the direction which has become its own through the transmission of centuries, that nation dies, if it succeeds in the attempt. And, therefore, if you succeed in the attempt to throw off your religion and take up either politics or society, or any other thing as your centre, as the vitality of your national life, the result will be, that you will become extinct. Give it up and you die; death will be the only result, annihilation the only effect, the moment you step beyond that life-current. Religion and religion alone is the life of India, and when that goes India will die, in spite of politics, in spite of social reforms, in spite of *Kuvera's* wealth poured upon the head of every one of her children. I do not mean to say that other things are not necessary. I do not mean to say that political or social improvements are not necessary, but what I mean is this, and I want you to bear it in mind, that they are secondary here, and that religion is primary.

When the life-blood is strong and pure no disease germ can live in that body. Our life-blood is spirituality. If it flows clear, if it flows strong and pure and vigorous, everything is right; political, social, any other material defects, even the poverty of the land, will all be cured if that blood is pure.

To take a simile from modern medicine, we know that there must be two causes to produce a disease, some poison germ outside, and the state of the body. Until the body is in a state to admit the germs, until the body is degraded to a lower vitality so that the germs may enter and thrive and multiply, there is no power in any germ in the world to produce a disease in the body. In fact, millions of germs are continually passing through everyone's body; but so long as it is vigorous it never is conscious of them. It is only when the body is weak that these germs take possession of it and produce disease. Just so with the national life. It is when the national body is weak that all sorts of disease germs, in the political state of the race or in its social state, in its educational or intellectual state, crowd into the system and produce disease.

To remedy it, therefore, we must go to the root of this disease and cleanse the blood of all impurities. The one tendency will be to strengthen the man, to make the blood pure, the body vigorous, so that it will be able to resist and throw off all external poisons. We have seen that our vigour, our strength, nay, our national life is in our religion. That is the life of our race and that must be strengthened.

You have withstood the shocks of centuries simply because you took great care of it, you sacrificed everything else for it. Your forefathers underwent everything boldly, even death itself, but preserved their religion. Temple after temple was broken down by the foreign conqueror, but no sooner had the wave passed than the spire of the temple rose up again. Some of these old temples of Southern India, and those like *Somnath* of Gujarat, will teach you volumes of wisdom, will give you a keener insight into the history of the race than any amount of books. Mark how these temples bear the marks of a hundred attacks and a hundred regenerations, continually destroyed and continually springing up out of the ruins, rejuvenated and strong as ever! That is the national mind, that is the national life-current. Follow it and it leads to glory.

The Indian mind is first religious, then anything else. So this is to be strengthened. You must make all and everything work through that vitality of your religion. Let all your nerves vibrate through the backbone of your religion. The national ideals of India are renunciation and service. Intensify her in those channels, and the rest will take care of itself. The banner of the spiritual cannot be raised too high in this country. In it alone is salvation.

The Indian nation cannot be killed. Deathless it stands, and it will stand so long as that spirit shall remain as the background, so long as her people do not give up their spirituality. Beggars they may remain, poor and poverty-stricken; dirt and squalor may surround them perhaps throughout all time, but let them not give up their God, let them not forget that they are the children of the sages.

Her Mission

Why did not this Hindu race die out, in the face of so many troubles and tumults of a thousand years? If our customs and manners are so very bad, how is it that we have not been effaced from the face of the earth by this time? Have the various foreign conquerors spared any pa ns to crush us out? Why, then, were not the Hindus blotted out of existence, as happened with men in other countries which are uncivilized? Why was not India depopulated and turned into a wilderness? Why, then foreigners would have lost no time to come and settle in

India, and till her fertile lands in the same way as they did and are still doing in America, Australia and Africa? First understand that India has strength as well, has a substantial reality of her own yet. Furthermore, understand that India is still living, because she has her own quota yet to give to the general store of the world's civilization.

Within every man, there is an idea; the external man is only the outward manifestation, the mere language of this idea within. Likewise, every nation has a corresponding national idea. This idea is working for the world and is necessary for its preservation. The day when the necessity of an idea as an element for the preservation of the world is over, that very day the receptacle of that idea, whether it be an individual or a nation, will meet destruction. The reason that we Indians are still living, in spite of so much misery, distress, poverty and oppression from within and without is that we have a national idea, which is yet necessary for the preservation of the world.

Each race has a peculiar bent, each race has a peculiar *raison d'être*, each race has a peculiar mission to fulfil in the life of the world. Each race has to make its own result, to fulfil its own mission. Political greatness or military power was never the mission of our race; it never was, and, mark my words, it never will be. But there has been the other mission given to us, which is to conserve, to preserve, to accumulate, as it were, into a dynamo, all the spiritual energy of the race, and that concentrated energy is to pour forth in a deluge on the world, whenever circumstances are propitious.

Sceptres have been broken and thrown away, the ball of power has passed from hand to hand; but in India, courts and kings always touched only a few; the vast mass of the people, from the highest to the lowest, has been left to pursue its own inevitable course, the current of national life flowing at times slow and half-conscious, at others, strong and awakened. I stand in awe before the unbroken procession of scores of shining centuries, with here and there a dim link in the chain, only to flare up with added brilliance in the next, and there she is walking with her own majestic steps—my motherland—to fulfil her glorious destiny, which no power on earth or in heaven can check—the regeneration of man the brute into man the God.

Aye, a glorious destiny, my brethren, for as far back as the days of the Upanishads we have thrown the challenge to the world—'*Na dhanena na prajayā tyāgenaike amritatwamānashuh*—not by wealth, not by progeny, but by renunciation alone immortality is reached.' Race after race has taken the challenge up, and tried their utmost to solve the world-riddle on the plane of desires. They have all failed in the past—the old ones have become extinct under the weight of wickedness and misery, which lust for power and gold brings in its train, and the new ones are tottering to their fall. The question has yet to be decided whether peace will survive or war; whether patience will survive or non-forbearance; whether goodness will survive or wickedness: whether muscle will survive or brain; whether worldliness will survive or spirituality. We have solved our problem ages ago and held on to it through good or evil fortune, and mean to hold on to it till the end of time. Our solution is unworldliness—renunciation.

This is the theme of Indian life-work, the burden of her eternal songs, the backbone of her existence, the foundation of her being, the *raison d'être* of her very existence—the spiritualization of the human race. In this her life-course she has never deviated, whether the Tartar ruled or the Turk, whether the Moghul ruled or the English.

For a complete civilization the world is waiting, waiting for the treasures to come out of India, waiting for the marvellous spiritual inheritance of the race, which, through decades of degradation and misery, the nation has still clutched to her breast. The world is waiting for that treasure; little do you know how much of hunger and of thirst there is outside of India for these wonderful treasures of our forefathers. We talk here, we quarrel with each other, we laugh at and ridicule everything holy. Little do we understand the heart-pangs of millions waiting outside the walls, stretching forth their hands for a little sip of that nectar which our forefathers have preserved in this land of India.

Her Future

Whether you believe in spirituality or not, for the sake of the national life, you have to get a hold on spirituality and keep to it. Then stretch the other hand out and gain all you can from other races, but everything must be subordinated to that one ideal of life; and out of that a wonderful, glorious, future India will come—I am sure it is coming—a greater India than ever was. Sages will spring up greater than all the ancient sages, and your ancestors will not only be satisfied, but I am sure, they will be proud, from their positions in other worlds, to look down upon their descendants, so glorious, and so great. Let us all work hard, my brethren, this is no time for sleep. On our work depends the coming of the India of the future. She is there ready waiting. She is only sleeping. Arise, and awake and see her seated here, on her eternal throne, rejuvenated, more glorious than she ever was—this motherland of ours.

A mighty tree produces a beautiful ripe fruit. That fruit falls on the ground, it decays and rots, and out of that decay springs the root and the future tree, perhaps mightier than the first one. This period of decay through which we have passed was all the more necessary. Out of this decay is coming the India of the future; it is sprouting, its first leaves are already out, and a mighty, gigantic tree is here, already beginning to appear.

The longest night seems to be passing away, the sorest trouble seems to be coming to an end at last, the seeming corpse appears to be awaking, and a voice is coming to us—away back where history and even tradition fails to peep into the gloom of the past, coming down from there, reflected, as it were, from peak to peak of the infinite *Himālaya* of knowledge, and of love, and of work, 'India, this motherland of ours'—a voice is coming unto us, gentle, firm, and yet unmistakable in its utterances, and is gaining volume as days pass by, and behold, the sleeper is awakening! Like a breeze from the Himalayas, it is bringing life into the almost dead bones and muscles, the lethargy is passing away, and only the blind cannot see, or the perverted will not see that she is awakening, this motherland of ours, from her deep long sleep. None can resist her any more; never is she going to sleep any more; no outward powers can hold her back any more; for the infinite giant is rising to her feet.

Up, up, the long night is passing, the day is approaching, the wave has risen, nothing will be able to resist its tidal fury. Believe, believe, the decree has gone forth, the fiat of the Lord has gone forth—India must rise, the masses and the poor are to be made happy. Rejoice! The flood of spirituality has risen. I see it is rolling over the land resistless, boundless, all-absorbing. Every man to the fore, every good will be added to its forces, every hand will smooth its way, and glory be unto the Lord!

CHAPTER II

PRESENT DECADENCE

Its Causes

We are to blame: We, as Vedantists, know for certain that there is no power in the universe to injure us unless we first injure ourselves. Let us blame none, let us blame our own *karma*. No bacilli can attack the human frame until it is degraded and degenerated by vice, bad food, privation, and exposure; the healthy man passes scatheless through masses of poisonous bacilli. The effect is here and the cause is here too. We are to blame. Stand up, be bold, and take the blame on your own shoulders. Do not go about throwing mud at others; for all the faults you suffer from, you are the sole and only cause.

Ignoring the past: Nowadays, everybody blames those who constantly look back to their past. It is said that so much looking back to the past is the cause of all India's woes. To me, on the contrary, it seems that the opposite is true. So long as they forgot the past, the Hindu nation remained in a state of stupor; and as soon as they have begun to look into their past, there is on every side a fresh manifestation of life.

Every critical student knows that the social laws of India have always been subject to great periodic changes. At their inception, these laws were the embodiment of a gigantic plan, which was to unfold itself slowly through time. The great seers of ancient India saw so far ahead of their time, that the world has to wait centuries yet to appreciate their wisdom, and it is this very inability, on the part of their own descendants, to appreciate the full scope of this wonderful plan, that is the one and only cause of the degeneration of India.

Narrowing our outlook: We find that one of the causes which led to this degeneration was the narrowing of our view, narrowing the scope of our actions. That we did not go out to compare things with other nations, did not mark the workings that have been all around us, has been the one great cause of this degradation of the Indian mind.

One of the great causes of India's misery and downfall has been that she narrowed herself, went into her shell, as the oyster does, and refused to give her jewels and her treasures to the other races of mankind, refused to give the life-giving truths to thirsting nations outside the Aryan fold. I am thoroughly convinced that no individual or nation can live by holding itself apart from the community of others, and whenever such an attempt has been made under false ideas of greatness, policy or holiness—the result has always been disastrous to the secluding one. To my mind, the one great cause of the downfall and the degeneration of India was the building of a wall of custom, whose foundation was hatred of others, round the nation, and the real aim of which in ancient times was to prevent the Hindus from coming in contact with the surrounding Buddhistic nations. Whatever cloak ancient or modern sophistry may try to throw over it, the inevitable result—the vindication of the moral law, that none can hate others without degenerating himself—is that the race that was foremost amongst the ancient races is now a byword, and a scorn among nations. We are object-lessons of the violation of that law which our ancestors were the first to discover and disseminate.

Perversion of religion: A country, the big leaders of which have for the past two thousand years been only discussing whether to take food with the right hand or the left, whether to take water from the right-hand side or from the left—if such a country does not go to ruin what else will? Think of the last six hundred or seven hundred years of degeneration, when grown-up men by the hundreds have been discussing for years, whether we should drink a glass of water with the right hand or the left, whether the hand should be washed three times or four times, whether we should gargle five or six times. What can you expect from men who pass their lives in discussing such momentous questions as these, and writing most learned philosophies on them!

There is a danger of our religion getting into the kitchen. We are neither Vedantists, most of us now, nor Pauranics, nor Tantrics. We are just "don't-touchists". Our religion is in the kitchen. Our God is the cooking-pot, and our religion is "Don't touch me, I am holy". If this goes on for another century, every one of us will be in a lunatic asylum. It is a sure sign of softening of the brain when the mind cannot grasp the higher problems of life; all originality is lost, the mind has lost all its strength, its activity, and its power of thought, and just tries to go round and round the smallest curve it can find.

Tyranny over the masses: I consider that the great

national sin is the neglect of the masses, and that is one of the causes of her downfall. No amount of politics would be of any avail until the masses in India are once more well educated, well fed, and well cared for. They pay for our education, they build our temples, but in return they get kicks. They are practically our slaves. If we want to regenerate India, we must work for them.

Neglect of women: "The gods are pleased where the women are held in esteem", says the old Manu. We are horrible sinners, and our degradation is due to our calling women 'despicable worms', 'gateways to hell', and so forth. The Lord has said, "Thou art the woman, Thou art the man, Thou art the boy and the girl as well". And we on our part are crying, "Who has made the bewitching woman?"

It is very difficult to understand why in this country so much difference is made between men and women, whereas the Vedanta declares that one and the same conscious Self is present in all beings. You always criticise the women, but say, what have you done for their uplift? Writing down Smritis, etc., and binding them by hard rules, the men have turned the women into mere manufacturing machines! If you do not raise the women who are the living embodiment of the Divine Mother, don't think that you have any other way to rise.

Its Symptoms and Cure

Cultural heresy and fanaticism: In our sight, here in India, there are several dangers. Of these, the two, Scylla and Charybdis, rank materialism and its opposite, arrant superstition, must be avoided.

There is the man today who after drinking the cup of Western wisdom, thinks that he knows everything. He laughs at the ancient sages. All Hindu thought to him is arrant trash, philosophy, mere child's prattle, and religion, the superstition of fools.

Imitation is not civilisation. I may deck myself out in a Raja's dress; but will that make me a Raja? An ass in a lion's skin never makes a lion. Imitation, cowardly imitation, never makes for progress. It is verily the sign of awful degradation in a man. Aye, when a man has begun to hate himself, then the last blow has come. When a man has begun to be ashamed of his ancestors, the end has come. Do not be dragged away out of this Indian life; do not for a moment think that it will be better for India if all the Indians dressed, ate and behaved like another race.

On the other hand, there is the man educated, but a sort of monomaniac, who runs to the other extreme, and wants to explain the omen of this and that. He has philosophical and metaphysical, and Lord knows what other puerile explanations for every superstition that belongs to this peculiar race, or his peculiar gods, or his peculiar village. Every little village superstition is to him a mandate of the Vedas, and upon the carrying out of it, according to him, depends the national life. You must beware of this.

The fact is that we have many superstitions, many bad spots and sores on our body—these have to be excised, cut off, and destroyed—but these do not destroy our religion, our national life, our spirituality. Every principle of religion is safe, and the sooner these black spots are purged away, the better the principles will shine, the more gloriously. Stick to them.

Physical weakness: In spite of the greatness of the Upanishads, in spite of our boasted ancestry of sages, compared to many other races, I must tell you that we are weak, very weak. First of all, is our physical weakness. That physical weakness is the cause at least of one-third of our miseries.

Our young men must be strong. Religion will come afterwards. Be strong, my young friends; that is my advice to you. You will be nearer to Heaven through football than through the study of the Gita. You will understand Gita better with your biceps, your muscles, a little stronger. You will understand the mighty genius and the mighty strength of Krishna better with a little of strong blood in you. You will understand the Upanishads better and the glory of the Atman, when your body stands firm upon your feet, and you feel yourselves as men. What I want is muscles of iron and nerves of steel, inside which dwells a mind of the same material as that of which the thunderbolt is made. Strength, manhood, *Kshātra-virya* plus *Brahmateja*.

Lack of faith in ourselves: We have lost faith. Would you believe me, we have less faith than the Englishman and woman, a thousand times less faith! Why is it that we three hundred and thirty millions of people, have been ruled for the last one thousand years by any and every handful of foreigners who chose to walk over our prostrate bodies? Because they had faith in themselves and we had not. We want *shraddhā*, we want faith in our own selves. Strength is life, weakness is death.

Being a conquered race, we have brought ourselves to believe that we are weak and have no independence in anything. So, how can it be but that the *shraddhā* is lost? The idea of true *shraddhā* must be brought back once more to us, the faith in our own selves must be re-awakened, and, then only, all the problems which face our country will gradually be solved by ourselves.

Have faith in yourselves, and stand upon that faith and be strong; that is what we need. 'We are the Atman, deathless and free; pure, pure by nature. Can we ever commit any sin? Impossible! '—Such a faith is needed. Such a faith makes men of us, makes gods of us. Have faith that you are all born to do great things! Each one of us will have to believe that every one else in the world has done his work, and the only work remaining to be done to make the world perfect has to be done by himself. This is the responsibility we have to take upon ourselves. Give up the awful disease that is creeping into our national blood, that idea of ridiculing everything, that loss of seriousness. Give that up. Be strong and have this *shraddhā*, and everything else is bound to follow.

Lack of self-help: The whole national character is one of childish dependence. They are all ready to enjoy food if it is brought to their mouth, and even some want it pushed down. You do not deserve to live if you cannot help yourselves. You must always remember that every nation must save itself; so must every man; do not look to others for help. You must not depend on any foreign help. Nations, like individuals, must help themselves. This is real patriotism. If a nation cannot do that, its time has not yet come. It must wait.

Lack of obedience: Every one wants to command and no one wants to obey; this is owing to the absence of that wonderful *brahmacharya* system of yore. First, learn to obey. The command will come by itself. Always first learn to be a servant, and then you will be fit to be a master. If your superior orders you to throw yourself into a river and catch a crocodile, you must first obey and then reason with him. Even if the order be wrong, first obey and then contradict it. Cultivate the virtue of obedience, but you must not sacrifice your own faith. No centralisation is possible unless there is obedience to superiors. No great work can be done without this centralisation of individual forces.

Laziness, selfishness and jealousy: There is too much talk, talk, talk! we are great, we are great! Nonsense! We are imbeciles; that is what we are! We speak of many things, parrot-like, but never do them; speaking and not doing has become a habit with us. This sort of weak brain is not able to do anything; we must strengthen it.

We are lazy; we cannot work; we cannot combine; we do not love each other; we are intensely selfish; not three of us can come together without hating each other, without being jealous of each other. That is the state in which we are—hopelessly disorganised mobs, immensely selfish, fighting each other for centuries as to whether a certain mark is to be put on our forehead this way or that way; writing volumes and volumes upon such momentous questions as to whether the look of a man spoils my food or not!

Lack of organizing capacity: The faculty of organisation is entirely absent in our nature, but this has to be infused. The great secret is—absence of jealousy. Be always ready to concede to the opinions of your brethren, and try always to conciliate. Why is it that organisations are so powerful? Why is it, to take a case in point, that forty millions of Englishmen rule three hundred millions of people here? What is the psychological explanation? These forty millions put their wills together and that means infinite power, and you three hundred millions have a will each separate from the other. Therefore to make a great future of India, the whole secret lies in organisation, accumulation of power, co-ordination of wills. Already before my mind rises one of the marvellous verses of the *Atharva Veda Samhitā* which says, "Be thou all of one mind, be thou all of one thought, for in the days of yore, the gods being of one mind were enabled to receive oblations. That the gods can be worshipped by men is because they are of one mind." Being of one mind is the secret of society. And the more you go on fighting and quarrelling about all trivialities such as "Dravidian" and "Aryan", and the question of Brāhmanas and non-Brāhmanas and all that the further you are off from that accumulation of energy and power which is going to make the future India. For mark you, the future India depends entirely upon that. This is the secret, accumulation of will-power, co-ordination, bringing them all, as it were, into one focus.

Lack of business integrity: The Hindus have a peculiar slovenliness in business matters, not being sufficiently methodical and strict in keeping accounts, etc. All combined efforts in India sink under the weight of one iniquity—we have not yet developed strict business principles. Business is business, in the highest sense, and no friendship—or as the Hindu proverb says "eye-shame"—should be there. One should keep the clearest account of everything in one's charge—and never, never apply the funds intended for one thing to any other use whatsoever—even if one starves the next moment. This is business integrity. Next, energy unfailing. Whatever you do let that be your worship for the time being.

Lack of love: No man, no nation can hate others and live. India's doom was sealed the very day they invented the word *mlechchha* and stopped from communion with others. Love never fails; today or tomorrow or ages after, truth will conquer. Love shall win the victory. Do you love your fellow-men?

Charge to National Workers

Where should you go to seek for God—are not all the poor, the miserable, the weak, gods? Why not worship them first? Why go to dig a well on the shores of the Ganga? Believe in the omnipotent power of love. Have you love?—You are omnipotent. Are you perfectly unselfish? If so, you are irresistible. It is character that pays everywhere. It is the Lord who protects His children in the depths of the sea. Your country requires heroes: be heroes!

Feel from the heart. What is in the intellect or reason? It goes a few steps and there it stops. But through the heart comes inspiration. Love opens the most impossible gates; love is the gate to all the secrets of the universe. Feel, therefore, my would-be reformers, my would-be patriots! Do you feel? Do you feel that millions and millions of the descendants of gods and of sages have become next-door neighbours to brutes? Do you feel that millions are starving today, and millions have been starving for ages? Do you feel that ingorance has come over the land as a dark cloud? Does it make you restless? Does it make you sleepless? Has it gone into your blood, coursing through your veins, becoming constant with your heart-beats? Has it made you almost mad? Are you seized with that one idea of the misery of ruin, and have you forgotten all about your name, your fame, your wives, your children, your property, even your own bodies? Have you done that? That is the first step to become a patriot, the very first step.

Come out of your narrow holes and have a look abroad. See how nations are on the march! Do you love man? Do you love your country? Then come, let us struggle for higher and better things; look not back, no, not even if you see the dearest and nearest cry. Look not back, but forward!

Men, men—these are wanted: everything else will be ready, but strong, vigorous, believing young men, sincere to the backbone, are wanted. A hundred such and the world becomes revolutionized.

The essential thing is renunciation—without renunciation none can pour out his whole heart in working for others. The man of renunciation sees all with an equal eye, and devotes himself to the service of all. Nothing will be able to resist truth and love and sincerity. Are you sincere, unselfish even unto death, and loving? Then fear not, not even death. As you go on your way serving others, you will, on a parallel line, advance in the path of knowledge. Work, work the idea, my brave, noble, good souls—to the wheel, to the wheel put your shoulders! Stop not to look back for name, or fame, or any such nonsense. Throw self overboard and work.

Down with all sloth, down with all enjoyments here or hereafter. Plunge into the fire and bring the people towards the Lord. Put yourself to work, and you will find such tremendous power coming to you that you will feel it hard to bear. Even the least work done for others awakens the power within; even thinking the least good of others gradually instils into the heart the strength of a lion. I love you all ever so much, but I would wish you all to die working for others—I should be rather glad to see you do that!

Truth is infinitely more weighty than untruth; so is goodness. If you possess these, they will make their way by sheer gravity. Every work has got to pass through hundreds of difficulties before succeeding. Those that persevere will see the light, sooner or later. Infinite patience, infinite purity, and infinite perseverance are the secret of success in a good cause. Hold on with faith and strength; be true, be honest, be pure. Do not figure out big plans at first, but begin slowly, feel your ground and proceed, up and up.

Take care of these two things—love of power and jealousy. Nobody will come to help you, if you put yourself forward as a leader. Kill self first if you want to succeed. Do not try to lead your brethren, but serve them. The brutal mania for leading has sunk many a great ship in the waters of life. Take care specially of that. Never attempt to guide or rule others, or, as the Yankees say, "boss" others. Be the servant of all. Do not try to be a ruler. He is the best ruler who can serve well.

Be patient with everybody. Why should you mix in controversies? Bear with the various opinions of everybody. Patience, purity, and perseverance will prevail. Please everybody without becoming a hypocrite and without being a coward. Hold on to your own ideas with strength and purity, and whatever obstructions may now be in your way, the world is bound to listen to you in the long run. Be positive; do not criticise others. Give your message, teach what you have to teach, and there stop. The Lord knows the rest.

Expand your hearts and hopes, as wide as the world. I want the intensity of the fanatic plus the extensity of the materialist. Deep as the ocean, broad as the infinite sky, that is the sort of heart we want.

We are poor, my brothers, we are nobodies, but such have been always the instruments of the Most High. Do not care for anybody to help you. Is not the Lord infinitely greater than all human help? Be holy—trust in the Lord, depend on Him always, and you are on the right track; nothing can prevail against you. Let us pray "Lead, Kindly Light"—a beam will come through the dark, and a hand will be stretched forth to lead us. Glory unto the Lord—march on, the Lord is our General. Do not look back to see who falls—forward—onward! Thus and thus we shall go on, brethren. One falls, and another takes up the work. Work on, brave hearts, fail not—no saying nay; work on—the Lord is behind the work. *Mahāshakti* is with you.

CHAPTER III

ESSENTIALS FOR REGENERATION

Training Sincere Workers

The basis of all systems, social or political, rests upon the goodness of men. No nation is great or good because Parliament enacts this or that, but because its men are great and good. Men are more valuable than all the wealth of the world.

All that England can do is to help India to work out her own salvation. All progress at the dictation of another, whose hand is at India's throat, is valueless in my opinion. The highest work can only degenerate when slave-labour produces it. Tell me, whose wants are those—yours or the ruler's? If yours, will the ruler supply them for you, or will you have to do that for yourselves? Never are the wants of a beggar fulfilled. Suppose the Government give you all you need, where are the men who are able to keep up the things demanded? So make men first.

When you have men who are ready to sacrifice their everything for their country, sincere to the backbone—when such men arise, India will become great in every respect. Then only will India awake, when hundreds of large-hearted men and women giving up all desires of enjoying the luxuries of life, will long and exert themselves to their utmost, for the well-being of the millions of their countrymen who are gradually sinking lower and lower in the vortex of destitution and ignorance.

Work among those young men who can devote heart and soul to this one duty—the duty of raising the masses of India. Awake them, unite them, and inspire them with this spirit of renunciation; it depends wholly on the young people of India. A hundred thousand men and women, fired with the zeal of holiness, fortified with eternal faith in the Lord, and nerved to lion's courage by their sympathy for the poor and the fallen and the downtrodden, will go over the length and breadth of the land, preaching the gospel of salvation, the gospel of help, the gospel of social raising-up—the gospel of equality.

What I now want is a band of fiery missionaries. My plan is to start institutions in India, to train our young men as preachers of the truths of our Scriptures, in India and outside India.

Deluging the Land with Spiritual Ideals

The political systems that we are struggling for in India have been in Europe for ages, have been tried for centuries, and have been found wanting. One after another, the institutions, systems, and everything connected with political government have been condemned as useless, and Europe is restless, does not know where to turn. It is hopeless and perfectly useless to attempt to govern mankind with the sword. You will find that the very centres from which such ideas as government by force sprang up, are the very first centres to degrade and degenerate and crumble to pieces. Europe, the centre of the manifestation of material energy, will crumble into dust within fifty years, if she is not mindful to change her position, to shift her ground and make spirituality the basis of her life.

Everything goes to show that socialism or some form of rule by the people, call it what you will, is coming on the boards. The people will certainly want the satisfaction of their material needs, less work, no oppression, no war, more food. What guarantee have we that this, or any civilisation, will last, unless it is based on religion, on the goodness of man? Depend on it, religion goes to the root of the matter. If it is right, all is right.

One must admit that law, government, politics are phases not final in any way. There is a goal beyond them where law is not needed. Christ saw that the basis is not law, that morality and purity are the only strength. You have the saying that men cannot be made virtuous by an Act of Parliament. And that is why religion is of deeper importance than politics, since it goes to the root, and deals with the essentials of conduct.

I claim that no destruction of religion is necessary to improve the Hindu society, and that this state of society exists not on account of religion but because that religion has not been applied to society as it should have been. This I am ready to prove from our old books, every word of it. This is what I teach, and this is what we must struggle all our lives to carry out. The first work that demands our attention is that the most wonderful truths confined in our Upanishads, in our Scriptures, in our Puranas—must be brought out from the books and scattered broadcast all over the land. Every improvement in India requires first of all an upheaval in religion. Before flooding India with socialistic or political ideas, first deluge the land with spiritual ideas. In this land of charity, let us take up the energy of the first charity, the diffusion of spiritual knowledge. And that diffusion should not be confined within the bounds of India. After preaching spiritual knowledge, along with it will come that secular knowledge and every other knowledge that you want; but if you attempt to get the secular knowledge without religion, I tell you plainly, vain is your attempt in India, it will never have a hold on the people.

The first plank in the making of a future India, the first step that is to be hewn out of that rock of ages, is the unification of religion. All of us have to be taught that we Hindus have certain common ideas behind us, and that the time has come when for the well-being of ourselves, for the well-being of our race, we must give up all our little quarrels and differences. National union in India must be a gathering up of its scattered spiritual forces. A nation in India must be a union of those whose hearts beat to the same spiritual tune.

What our country now wants, are muscles of iron and nerves of steel, gigantic wills which nothing can resist, which can penetrate into the mysteries and the secrets of the universe, and will accomplish their purpose in any fashion, even if it meant going down to the bottom of the ocean and meeting death face to face. That is what we want, and that can only be created, established and strengthened, by understanding and realising the ideal of the Advaita, that ideal of the oneness of all. None can regenerate this land of ours without the practical application and effective operation of this ideal of the oneness of things. The truths of the Upanishads are before you. Take them up, live up to them, and the salvation of India will be at hand.

Let me tell you that we want strength, strength, and every time strength. And the Upanishads are the great mine of strength. Therein lies strength enough to invigorate the whole world; the whole world can be vivified, made strong, energised through them. They will call with trumpet voice upon the weak, the miserable, and the downtrodden of all races, all creeds, and all sects, to stand on their feet and be free; freedom, physical freedom, mental freedom, and spiritual freedom are the watchwords of the Upanishads.

If there is one word that you find coming out like a bomb from the Upanishads bursting like a bomb-shell upon masses of ignorance, it is the word, fearlessness. And the only religion that ought to be taught, is the religion of fearlessness. Arise, awake! Awake from this hypnotism of weakness. None is really weak; the soul is infinite, omnipotent, and omniscient. Stand up, assert yourself, proclaim the God within you, do not deny Him! Too much of inactivity, too much of weakness, too much of hypnotism, has been and is upon our race. O ye modern Hindus, de-hypnotise yourselves. Teach yourselves, teach everyone his real nature, call upon the sleeping soul and see how it awakes. Power will come, glory will come, goodness will come, purity will come, and everything that is excellent will come when this sleeping soul is roused to self-conscious activity.

Ever tell yourself—"I am He". These are the words

that will burn up the dross that is in the mind, words that will bring out the tremendous energy which is within you already, the infinite power which is sleeping in your heart.

All the social upheavalists, at least the leaders of them, are trying to find that all their communistic or equalising theories must have a spiritual basis, and that spiritual basis is Vedanta only. No amount of force or government, or legislative cruelty will change the conditions of a race, but it is spiritual culture and ethical culture alone that can change wrong racial tendencies for the better. Go back, go back to old age, when there was strength and vitality. Be strong once more, drink deep of the fountain of yore, and that is the only condition of life in India.

SOCIAL REFORM—ITS METHOD

Platform speeches have been made by the thousand, denunciations in volumes after volumes have been hurled upon the devoted head of the Hindu race and its civilization, and yet no good practical result has been achieved; and where is the reason for that? The reason is not hard to find. It is in the denunciation itself. Denunciation is not at all the way to do good.

Have no word of condemnation, even for the most superstitious and the most irrational of its institutions, for they also must have served some good in the past. Remember always that there is not in the world any other country whose institutions are really better in their aims and objects than the institutions of this land. Even those customs that are now appearing to be positive evils, have been positively life-giving in time past, and if we have to remove these, we must not do so with curses, but with blessings and gratitude for the glorious work these customs have done for the preservation of our race.

I do not believe in reform; I believe in growth. I do not dare to put myself in the position of God and dictate to our society, "This way thou shouldst move and not that." My ideal is growth, expansion, development on national lines. Each individual has to work out his own salvation; there is no other way, and so also nations. Until higher institutions have been evolved any attempt to break the old ones will be disastrous. Growth is always gradual. Take man where he stands and from thence give him a lift.

I am sorry to say that most of our modern reform-movements have been inconsiderate imitations of Western means and methods of work, and that surely will not do for India. All the reformers in India made the serious mistake of holding religion accountable for all the horrors of priestcraft and degeneration, and went forthwith to pull down the indestructible structure, and what was the result? Failure!

You must go down to the basis of the thing, to the very root of the matter. That is what I call radical reform. Put the fire there and let it burn upwards and make an Indian nation. My method of treatment is to take out by the roots the very causes of the disease and not keep them merely suppressed.

All healthy social changes are the manifestations of the spiritual forces working within, and if these are strong and well adjusted, society will arrange itself accordingly. Meddle not with so-called social reform for there cannot be any reform without spiritual reform first.

We do stand in need of social reform. At times great men would evolve new ideas of progress, and kings would give them the sanction of law. Thus social improvements had been in the past made in India, and in modern times to effect such progressive reforms, we will have first to build up such an authoritative power. Kings having gone, the power is the people's. We have, therefore, to wait till the people are educated, till they understand their needs and are ready and able to solve their problems. The tyranny of the minority is the worst tyranny in the world. Therefore, instead of frittering away our energies on ideal reforms, which will never become practical, we had better go to the root of the evil and make a legislative body, that is to say, educate our people so that they may be able to solve their own problems. Until that is done all these ideal reforms will remain ideals only. The new order of things is the salvation of the people by the people, and it takes time to make it workable, especially in India, which has always in the past been governed by kings.

If you wish to be a true reformer three things are necessary. The first to feel; do you really feel for your brothers? Do you really feel that there is so much misery in the world, so much ignorance and superstition? Do you really feel that men are your brothers? Does this idea come into your whole being? Does it run with your blood? Does it tingle in your veins? Does it course through every nerve and filament of your body? Are you full of that idea of sympathy? If you are, that is only the first step. You must think next if you have found any remedy. The old ideas may be all superstition—but in and round these masses of superstition are nuggets of gold and truth. Have you discovered the means by which to keep that gold alone, without any of the dross? One more thing is necessary. What is your motive? Are you sure that you are not actuated by greed of gold, by thirst for fame or power?

CHAPTER IV

EDUCATION: THE PANACEA OF ALL SOCIAL EVILS

The Present System

The education that you are getting now has some good points, but it has a tremendous disadvantage which is so great that the good things are all weighed down. In the first place it is not a man-making education, it is merely and entirely a negative education. A negative education or any training that is based on negation, is worse than death. The child is taken to school, and the first thing he learns is that his father is a fool, the second thing that his grandfather is a lunatic, the third thing that all his teachers are hypocrites, the fourth, that all the sacred books are lies! By the time he is sixteen he is a mass of negation, lifeless and boneless. And the result is, that fifty years of such education has not produced one original man in the three presidencies. Every man of originality that has been produced has been educated elsewhere, and not in this country, or they have gone to the old universities once more to cleanse themselves of superstitions.

We have had a negative education all along from our boyhood. We have only learnt that we are nobodies. Seldom are we given to understand that great men were ever born in our country. Nothing positive has been taught to us. We do not even know how to use our hands and feet! We have learnt only weakness.

The present system is nothing but a perfect machine for turning out clerks. I would even thank my stars if that were all. But no! See how men are becoming destitute of *shraddhā* and faith. They assert that the *Gītā* was only an interpolation and that the Vedas were but rustic songs! They like to master every detail concerning things and nations outside of India, but if you ask them they do not know even the names of their own forefathers up to the seventh generation, not to speak of the fourteenth!

Our pedagogues are making parrots of our boys, and ruining their brains by cramming a lot of subjects into them. Goodness gracious! What a fuss and fury about graduating, and after a few days all cooled down! And after all that, what is it they learn but that what religion and customs we have are all bad and what the Westerners have are all good! At last, they cannot keep the wolf from the door! What does it matter if this higher education remains or goes? It would be better if the people got a little technical education so that they might find work and earn their bread, instead of dawdling about and crying for service.

Is that education, as a result of which the will being continuously choked by force through generations, is now well-nigh killed out; under whose sway, why mention new ideas, even the old ones are disappearing one by one—is that education which is slowly making man a machine? It is more blessed, in my opinion, even to go wrong impelled by one's free will and intelligence than to be good as an automaton.

Well, you consider a man as educated if only he can pass some examinations and deliver good lectures. The education which does not help the common mass of people to equip themselves for the struggle for life, which does not bring out strength of character, a spirit of philanthropy, and the courage of a lion—is it worth the name? The education that you are receiving now in schools and colleges is only making you a race of dyspeptics. You are working like machines merely, and living a jelly-fish existence.

TRUE EDUCATION

What is education? Is it book-learning? No. Is it diverse knowledge? Not even that. The training by which the current and expression of will are brought under control and become fruitful, is called education. ....(True education) may be described as a development of faculty, not an accumulation of words, or, as a training of individuals to will rightly and efficiently.

The ideal of all education, all training should be man-making. Education is not the amount of information that is put into your brain and runs riot there, undigested, all your life. We must have life-building, man-making, character-making, assimilation of ideas. If you have assimilated five ideas and made them your life and character, you have more education than any man who has got by heart a whole library. "The ass carrying its load of sandal-wood knows only the weight and not the value of sandal-wood." If education is identical with information, the libraries are the greatest sages in the world, and encyclopædias are the *rishis*.

By education I do not mean the present system, but something in the line of positive teaching. Mere book-learning won't do. We want that education by which character is formed, strength of mind is increased, the intellect is expanded, and by which one can stand on one's own feet. What we want are Western science coupled with Vedanta, *brahmacharya* as the guiding motto, and also *shraddhā* and faith in one's own self.

Does higher education mean mere study of material sciences and turning out things of everyday use by machinery? The use of higher education is to find out how to solve the problems of life, and this is what is engaging the profound thought of the modern civilized world, but it was solved in our country thousands of years ago.

Education is the manifestation of the perfection already in man. I look upon religion as the innermost core of education. Mind, I do not mean my own, or any one else's opinion about religion. Religion is as the rice, and everything else, like the curries. Taking only curries causes indigestion, and so is the case with taking rice alone.

Ideal Method

Concentration and Detachment: We have but one method of acquiring knowledge. From the lowest man to the highest *yogin*, all have to use the same method; and that method is what is called concentration. The chemist in his laboratory concentrates all the energies of his mind into one focus, and throws them upon the materials he is analysing, and so finds out their secrets. The astronomer concentrates all the energies of his mind and projects them through his telescope upon the skies; and the stars, the sun, and the moon, give up their secrets to him.

How has all the knowledge in the world been gained but by the concentration of the powers of the mind? The world is ready to give up its secrets if we only know how to knock, how to give it the necessary blow. The strength and the force of the blow come through concentration. There is no limit to the power of the human mind. The more concentrated it is, the more power is brought to bear on one point; that is the secret.

Even the lowest shoeblack, if he gives more concentration will black shoes better; the cook with concentration will cook a meal all the better. In making money, or in worshipping God, or in doing anything, the stronger the power of concentration, the better will that thing be done. This is the one call, the one knock, which opens the gates of nature, and lets out floods of light. This, the power of concentration is the only key to the treasure-house of knowledge.

Along with the development of concentration we must develop the power of detachment. We must learn not only to attach the mind to one thing exclusively, but also to detach it at a moment's notice and place it upon something else. These two should be developed together to make it safe.

This is the systematic development of the mind. To me the very essence of education is concentration of mind, not the collecting of facts. If I had to do my education over again and had any voice in the matter, I would not study facts at all. I would develop the power of concentration and detachment, and then with a perfect instrument I could collect facts at will. Side by side, in the child, should be developed the power of concentration and detachment.

Brahmacharya: Every boy should be trained to practise absolute *brahmacharya* and then and then alone, faith and *shraddhā* will come. Chastity in thought, word and deed always and in all conditions is what is called *brahmacharya*. It is owing to want of continence that everything is on the brink of ruin in our country. By observance of strict *brahmacharya* all learning can be mastered in a very short time; one acquires an unfailing memory of what one hears or knows but once. The chaste brain has tremendous energy and gigantic willpower. Controlled desire leads to the highest results. Transform the sexual energy into the spiritual energy. The stronger the force is, the more can be done with it. Only a powerful current of water can do hydraulic mining.

Shraddhā: The idea of true *shraddhā* must be brought back once more to us. What makes the difference between man and man is the difference in the *shraddhā* and nothing else. What makes one man great and another weak and low is this *shraddhā*. No good comes out of the man who day and night thinks that he is nobody. If a man day and night thinks that he is miserable, low and nothing, nothing he becomes. We are children of the Almighty, we are sparks of the infinite, divine Fire. How can we be nothings? We are everything, ready to do everything; we can do everything. This faith in themselves was in the heart of our ancestors; this faith in themselves was the motive power that pushed them forward in the march of civilization. If there has been degeneration, if there has been defect, you will find that degeneration to have started on the day our people lost this faith in themselves. Therefore, teach this life-saving, great, ennobling, grand doctrine to your children, even from their very birth.

Character: What you want is character, strengthening of the will. Continue to exercise your will and it will take you higher. The will is almighty. It is character that can cleave through adamantine walls of difficulties. The character of any man is but the aggregate of his tendencies, the sum total of the bent of his mind. We are what our thoughts have made us. Thoughts live; they travel far. And so take care of what you think. Every work that we do, every movement of the body, every thought that we think, leaves an impression on the mind-stuff. What we are every moment is determined by the sum total of these impressions on the mind. Every man's character is determined by the sum total of these impressions. If good impressions prevail, the character becomes good, if bad, it becomes bad.

When a large number of these impressions is left on the mind they coalesce, and become a habit. The only remedy for bad habits is counter-habits; all the bad habits that have left their impressions are to be controlled by good habits. Go on doing good, thinking holy thoughts continuously; that is the only way to suppress base impressions.

Good and evil have an equal share in moulding character, and in some cases misery is a great teacher than happiness. In studying the great characters that the world has produced, I dare say, in the vast majority of cases, it will be found that it was misery that taught more than happiness, it was poverty that taught more than wealth, and it was blows that brought out their inner fire more than praise. Brought up in the lap of luxury, lying on a bed of roses and shedding a tear, who has become great?

Communion with Nature: Haven't you read the stories from the Upanishads? I will tell you one. Satyakāma went to live the life of a *brahmachārin* with his *guru*. The *guru* gave into his charge some cows and sent him away to the forest with them. Many months passed by, and when Satyakāma saw that the number of cows was doubled he thought of returning to his *guru*. When the disciple came back, the *guru* at once saw by a mere glance at his face that the disciple had learnt the knowledge of the Supreme Brahman. Now, the moral this story is meant to teach is that true education is gained by constant living in communion with Nature.

Gurukula system: My idea of education is *gurugrihavāsa*. Without the personal life of the teacher there would be no education. One should live from his very boyhood with one whose character is like a blazing fire, and should have before him a living example of the highest teaching. In our country the imparting of knowledge has always been through men of renunciation. The charge of imparting knowledge should again fall upon the shoulders of *tyāgis*.

The old system of education in India was very different from the modern system. The students had not to pay. It was thought that knowledge is so sacred that no man ought to sell it. Knowledge should be given freely and without any price. The teachers used to take students without charge and not only so, most of them gave their students food and clothes. To support these teachers, the wealthy families made gifts to them and they in their turn had to maintain their students. The teacher must not teach with any ulterior selfish motive, for money, name, or fame; his work must be simply out of love, out of pure love for mankind at large.

The disciple of old used to repair to the hermitage of the *guru*, fuel in hand, and the *guru*, after ascertaining his competence, would teach him the Vedas. Without faith, humility, submission and veneration in our hearts towards the teacher, there cannot be any growth in us. In those countries which have neglected to keep up this kind of relation, the teacher has become a mere lecturer, the teacher expecting his five dollars and the person taught expecting his brain to be filled with the teacher's words and each going his own way after this much is done.

The true teacher is he who can immediately come down to the level of the student, and transfer his soul to the student's soul and see through and understand through his mind. Such a teacher can really teach and none else. The conditions necessary for the taught are purity, a real thirst for knowledge, and perseverance. Purity in thought, speech and act is absolutely necessary. As to the thirst after knowledge, it is an old law that we all get whatever we want. None of us get anything other than what we fix our hearts upon. The student who sets out with a spirit of perseverance, will surely find success.

Psychological approach: Another thing that we want is the abolition of that system which aims at educating our boys in the same manner as that of the man who battered his ass, being advised that it could thereby be turned into a horse. You see no one can teach anybody. The teacher spoils everything by thinking that he is teaching. Vedānta says that within man is all knowledge—even in a boy it is so—and it requires only an awakening, and that much is the work of a teacher. You cannot teach a child any more than you can grow a plant. All you can do is on the negative side—you can only help. You can take away the obstacles, but knowledge comes out of its own nature. Loosen the soil a little, so that it may come out easily. Put a hedge round it; see that it is not killed by anything, and there your work stops. You cannot do anything else. The rest is a manifestation from within its own nature. So with the education of a child; a child educates itself.

Present Need and the Swami's Plan

What we need is to study, independent of foreign control, different branches of the knowledge that is our own, and with it the English language and Western science; we need technical education and all else which may develop industries, so that men, instead of seeking for service, may earn enough to provide for themselves, and save something against a rainy day.

We haven't even got a single book well suited for the

little boys. We must compile some books with short stories from the *Rāmāyana*, the *Mahābhārata*, and the Upanishads, etc., in very easy and simple language, and these are to be given to our little boys to read.

My whole ambition in life is to set in motion a machinery which will bring noble ideas to the door of everybody, and then let men and women settle their own fate. Let them know what our forefathers as well as other nations have thought on the most momentous questions of life. Let them see specially what others are doing now and then decide. We are to put the chemicals together, the crystallization will be done by nature according to her laws.

We must have a hold on the spiritual and secular education of the nation. You must dream it, you must talk it, you must think it, and you must work it out. Till then there is no salvation for the race. We must have the whole education of our country, spiritual and secular, in our hands, and it must be on national lines, through national methods, as far as practical. Of course this is a very big scheme, a very big plan. I do not know whether it will ever work out. But we must begin the work.

We must have a temple, for with the Hindus religion must come first. We will make it a non-sectarian temple, having only '*Om*', as the symbol, the greatest symbol, of any sect. Here should be taught the common grounds of our different sects, and at the same time the different sects should have perfect liberty to come and teach their doctrines, with only one restriction, that is, not to quarrel with other sects. Secondly, in connection with this temple there should be an institution to train teachers who must go about teaching religion and giving secular education to our people; as we have been already carrying religion from door to door, let us along with it carry secular education also. That can be easily done. Then the work will extend through these bands of teachers and preachers, and gradually we shall have similar temples in other places, until we have covered the whole of India. That is my plan. It may appear gigantic, but it is much needed.

CHAPTER V

UPLIFT OF THE MASSES

Their Worth

Our masses are very ignorant about secular things. Our masses are very good because poverty here is not a crime. Our masses are not violent. Many times I was near being mobbed in America and England, only on account of my dress. But I never heard of such a thing in India as a man being mobbed because of peculiar dress. In every other respect, our masses are much more civilized than the European masses. Experience teaches me that they are not dense, that they are not slow, that they are as eager and thirsty for information as any race under the sun.

Those uncared for lower classes of India—the peasants and weavers and the rest who have been conquered by foreigners and are looked down upon by their own people—it is they who from time immemorial have been working silently, without even getting the remuneration of their labours! The peasant, the shoemaker, the sweeper, and such other lower classes of India have much greater capacity for work and self-reliance than you. They have been silently working through long ages, and producing the entire wealth of the land, without a word of complaint.

Never mind if they have not read a few books like you, if they have not acquired your tailor-made civilization. What do these matter? But they are the backbone of a nation in all countries. If these lower classes stop work, where will you get your food, clothing from? If the sweepers of Calcutta stop work for a day, it creates a panic; and if they strike for three days, the whole town will be depopulated by the outbreak of epidemics. If the labourers stop work, your supply of food and clothes also stops. And you regard them as low-class people and vaunt about your own culture!

Ye labouring classes of India, as a result of your silent, constant labours Babylon, Persia, Alexandria, Greece, Rome, Venice, Genoa, Baghdad, Samarkand, Spain, Portugal, France, Denmark, Holland and England have successively attained supremacy and eminence! And you?—Well, who cares to think of you? Those whose heart's blood has contributed to all the progress that has been made in the world—well, who cares to praise them? The world-conquering heroes of spirituality, war and poetry are in the eyes of all, and they have received the homage of mankind; but where nobody looks, no one gives a word of encouragement, where everybody hates—that living amid such circumstances and displaying boundless patience, infinite love and dauntless practicality, our proletariat are doing their duty in their homes day and night, without the slightest murmur—well, is there no heroism in this? Many turn out to be heroes, when they have got some great task to perform. Even a coward easily gives up his life, and the most selfish man behaves disinterestedly, when there is a multitude to cheer them on, but blessed indeed is he who manifests the same unselfishness and devotion to duty in the smallest of acts, unnoticed by all—and it is you who are actually doing this, ye ever-trampled labouring classes of India! I bow to you.

Their Present Condition and Its Cause

Whether the leadership of society be in the hands of those who monopolise learning, or wield the power of riches or arms, the source of its power is always the subject masses. By so much as the class in power severs itself from this source, by so much is it sure to become weak. But such is the strange irony of fate, such is the queer working of *māyā*, that they from whom this power is directly or indirectly drawn, by fair means or foul—by deceit, stratagem, force, or by voluntary gift—they soon cease to be taken into account by the leading class.

In this country of ours, the very birth-place of the Vedānta, our masses have been hypnotised for ages. To touch them is pollution; to sit with them is pollution! Hopeless they were born; hopeless they must remain! And the result is that they have been sinking, sinking, sinking, and have come to the last stage to which a human being can come. For what country is there in the world where man has to sleep with the cattle? And for this, blame nobody else, do not commit the mistake of the ignorant. The effect is here and the cause is here too. We are to blame. Stand up, be bold, and take the blame on your own shoulders. Do not go about throwing mud at others; for all the faults you suffer from you are the sole and the only cause.

Our aristocratic ancestors went on treading the common masses of our country under foot, till they became helpless, till under this torment the poor, poor people nearly forgot that they were human beings. They have been compelled to be merely hewers of wood and drawers of water. The poor, the low, the sinner in India have no friends, no help—they cannot rise, try however they may. They sink lower and lower every day, they feel the blows showered upon them by a cruel society, and they do not know whence the blow comes. They have forgotten that they too are men. And the result is slavery.

Thoughtful people within the last few years have seen it, but unfortunately laid it at the door of the Hindu religion, and to them, the only way of bettering is by crushing this grandest religion of the world. Hear me, I have discovered the secret through the grace of the Lord. Religion is not at fault. On the other hand, your religion teaches you that every being is only your own self multiplied. But it was the want of practical application, the want of sympathy—the want of heart. The Lord once more came to you as Buddha and taught you how to feel, how to sympathise with the poor, the miserable, the sinner, but you heard Him not. And just as the Jews denied the Lord Jesus and are since that day wandering over the world as homeless beggars, tyrannised over by everybody, so you are bond-slaves to any nation that thinks it worth while to rule over you. Ah tyrants! you do not know that the obverse is tyranny, and the reverse, slavery. The slave and the tyrant are synonymous.

No religion on earth preaches the dignity of humanity in such a lofty strain as Hinduism, and no religion on earth treads upon the necks of the poor and the low in such a fashion as Hinduism. The Lord has shown me that religion is not at fault, but it is the Pharisees and the Sadducees in Hinduism, hypocrites, who invent all sorts of engines of tyranny. Who reduced the *bhangis* and the *pariahs* to their present degraded condition? Heartlessness in our behaviour and at the same time preaching wonderful Advaitism—is it not adding insult to injury? You have the greatest religion which the world ever saw, and you feed the masses with stuff and nonsense. You have the perennial fountain flowing, and you give them ditch-water. Your graduate would not touch a low-caste man, but is ready to get out of him the money for his education.

Its Remedy and Our Responsibility

Engrossed in the struggle for existence they had not the opportunity for the awakening of knowledge. They have worked so long uniformly like machines guided by human intelligence, and the clever educated section have taken the substantial part of the fruits of their labour. In every country this has been the case. But times have changed. The lower classes are gradually awakening to this fact and making a united front against this, determined to exact their legitimate dues. The masses of Europe and America have been the first to awaken and have already begun to fight. Signs of the awakening have shown themselves in India too, as is evident from the number of strikes among the lower classes nowadays. The upper classes will no longer be able to repress the lower, try they ever so much. The well-being of the higher classes now lies in helping the lower to get their legitimate rights.

There are possibilities, opportunities and hope for every individual in this country (i.e. America). Today he is poor, tomorrow he may become rich and learned and respected. Here every one is anxious to help the poor. In India there is a howling cry that we are very poor, but how many charitable associations are there for the well-being of the poor? How many people really weep for the sorrows and sufferings of the millions of poor in India? Are we men? What are we doing for their livelihood, for their improvement? We do not touch them, we avoid their company! Are we men?

Travelling through many cities of Europe and observing in them the comforts and education of even the poor people, there was brought to my mind the state of our own poor people and I used to shed tears. What made the difference? Education was the answer I got. Through education, faith in one's own self, and through faith in one's own self the inherent Brahman is waking up in them, while the Brahman in us is gradually becoming dormant.

In New York I used to observe the Irish colonists come—downtrodden, haggard-looking, destitute of all possessions at home, penniless and wooden-headed—with their only belongings, a stick and a bundle of rags hanging at the end of it, fright in their steps, alarm in their eyes. A different spectacle in six months—the man walks upright, his attire is changed. In his eyes and steps there is no more sign of fright. What is the cause? Our Vedānta says that that Irishman was kept surrounded by contempt in his own country—the whole of nature was telling him with one voice—"Pat, you have no more hope, you are born a slave and will remain so." Having been thus told from his birth, Pat believed in it and hypnotised himself that he was very low, and the Brahman in him shrank away. While no sooner had he landed in America than he heard the shout going up on all sides—"Pat, you are a man as we are, it is man who has done all, a man like you and me can do everything: have courage!" Pat raised his head and saw that it was so, the Brahman within woke up, nature herself spoke, as it were, "Arise, awake, and stop not till the goal is reached." (*Katha Up.*, 1.3.4)

From the day when education and culture, etc., began to spread gradually from patricians to plebeians, grew the distinction between the modern civilization as of Western countries, and the ancient civilization as of India, Egypt, Rome, etc. I see it before my eyes, a nation is advanced in proportion as education and intelligence spread among the masses. The chief cause of India's ruin has been the monopolising of the whole education and intelligence of the land, by dint of pride and royal authority, among a handful of men. If we are to rise again, we shall have to do it in the same way, that is, by spreading education among the masses. The remedy now is the spread of education. My idea is to bring to the door of the meanest, the poorest, the noble ideas that the human race has developed both in and out of India, and let them think for themselves.

Who will bring the light to them—who will travel from door to door bringing education to them? Let these people be your God—think of them, work for them, pray for them incessantly—the Lord will show you the way. Him I call a *mahātman* (great soul) whose heart bleeds for the poor, otherwise he is a *durātman* (wicked soul). Let us unite our wills in continued prayer for their good. We may die unknown, unpitied, unbewailed, without accomplishing anything—but not one thought will be lost. It will take effect, sooner or later. My heart is too full to express my feeling; you know it, you can imagine it. So long as the millions live in hunger and ignorance, I hold every man a traitor, who having been educated at their expense, pays not the least heed to them! I call those men who strut about in their finery, having got all their money by grinding the poor wretches, so long as they do not do anything for those two hundred millions who are now no better than hungry savages!

We have to give them secular education. We have to follow the plan laid down by our ancestors, that is, to bring all the ideals slowly down among the masses. Raise them slowly up, raise them to equality. Impart even secular knowledge through religion.

Your duty at present is to go from one part of the country to another, from village to village, and make the people understand that mere sitting about idly won't do any more. Make them understand their real condition and say, "O ye brothers, all arise! Awake! How much longer would you remain asleep!" Go and advise them how to improve their own condition, and make them comprehend the sublime truths of the *shāstras*, by presenting them in a lucid and popular way. So long the Brāhmanas have monopolised religion; but since they cannot hold their ground against the strong tide of time, go and take steps so that one and all in the land may get that religion. Impress upon their minds that they have the same right to religion as the Brāhmanas. Initiate all, even down to the *chandālas*, in these fiery *mantras*. Also instruct them in simple words, about the necessities of life, and in trade, commerce, agriculture, etc.

Preach the idea of elevating the masses by means of a central college, and bringing education as well as religion to the door of the poor by means of missionaries trained in this college. Suppose some disinterested *sannyāsins*, bent on doing good to others, go from village to village, disseminating education, and seeking in various ways to better the condition of all down to the *chandāla*, through oral teaching, and by means of maps, cameras, globes and such other accessories—can't that bring forth good in time? If the mountain does not come to Mahomet, Mahomet must go to the mountain. The poor are too poor to come to schools and *pāthsālās*.

Remember that the nation lives in the cottage. But, alas! nobody ever did anything for them. Our modern reformers are very busy about widow remarriage. Of course, I am a sympathiser in every reform, but the fate of a nation does not depend upon the number of husbands their widows get, but upon the condition of the masses. Can you raise them? Can you give them back their lost individuality without making them lose their innate spiritual nature? Can you become an Occidental of occidentals in your spirit of equality, freedom, working energy, and at the same time a Hindu to the very backbone in religious culture and instincts? This is to be done and we will do it.

CHAPTER VI

CASTE PROBLEM

Caste in Society and Not in Religion

Though our castes and our institutions are apparently linked with our religion, they are not so. These institutions have been necessary to protect us as a nation, and when this necessity for self-preservation will no more exist, they will die a natural death. In religion there is no caste. A man from the highest caste and a man from the lowest may become a monk in India and the two castes become equal. The caste system is opposed to the religion of the Vedānta.

Caste is a social custom, and all our great preachers have tried to break it down. From Buddhism downwards, every sect has preached against caste, and every time it has only riveted the chains. Beginning from Buddha down to Rammohan Ray, everyone made the mistake of holding caste to be a religious institution and tried to pull down religion and caste all together, and failed.

In spite of all the ravings of the priests, caste is simply a crystallised social institution, which after doing its service is now filling the atmosphere of India with its stench, and it can only be removed by giving back to the people their lost social individuality. Caste is simply the outgrowth of the political institutions of India; it is a hereditary trade guild. Trade competition with Europe has broken caste more than any teaching.

THE UNDERLYING IDEA OF THE CASTE SYSTEM

The older I grow, the better I seem to think of caste and such other time-honoured institutions of India. There was a time when I used to think that many of them were useless and worthless, but the older I grow, the more I seem to feel a difference in cursing any one of them, for each one of them is the embodiment of the experience of centuries.

A child of but yesterday, destined to die the day after tomorrow, comes to me and asks me to change all my plans and if I hear the advice of that baby and change all my surroundings according to his ideas I myself should be a fool, and no one else. Much of the advice that is coming to us from different countries is similar to this. Tell these wiseacres, "I will hear you when you have made a stable society yourselves. You cannot hold on to one idea for two days, you quarrel and fail; you are born like moths in the spring and die like them in five minutes. You come up like bubbles and burst like bubbles too. First form a stable society like ours. First make laws and institutions that remain undiminished in their power through scores of centuries. Then will be the time to talk on the subject with you, but till then, my friend, you are only a giddy child."

Caste is a very good thing. Caste is the plan we want to follow. What caste really is, not one in a million understands. There is no country in the world without caste. In India, from caste we reach to the point where there is no caste. Caste is based throughout on that principle. The plan in India is to make everybody Brāhmana, the Brāhmana being the ideal of humanity.

If you read the history of India you will find that attempts have always been made to raise the lower classes. Many are the classes that have been raised. Many more will follow till the whole will become Brāhmana. That is the plan.

Our ideal is the Brāhmana of spiritual culture and renunciation. By the Brāhmana ideal what do I mean? I mean the ideal Brāhmana-ness in which worldliness is altogether absent and true wisdom is abundantly present. That is the ideal of the Hindu race. Have you not heard how it is declared that he, the Brāhmana, is not amenable to law, that he has no law, that he is not governed by kings, and that his body cannot be hurt? That is perfectly true. Do not understand it in the light thrown upon it by interested and ignorant fools, but understand it in the light of the true and original Vedantic conception. If the Brāhmana is he who has killed all selfishness and who lives and works to acquire and propagate wisdom and the power of love—if a country is altogether inhabited by such Brāhmanas, by men and women who are spiritual and moral and good, is it strange to think of that country as being above and beyond all law? What police, what Military are necessary to govern them? Why should any one govern them at all? Why should they live under a government? They are good and noble, and they are the men of God; these are our ideal Brāhmanas, and we read that in the *Satya Yuga* there was only one caste, and that was the Brāhmana. We read in the *Mahābhārata* that the whole world was in the beginning peopled with Brāhmanas, and that as they began to degenerate they became divided into different castes, and that when the cycle turns round they will all go back to that Brāhmanical origin.

The son of a Brāhmana is not necessarily always a Brāhmana; though there is every possibility of his being one, he may not become so. The Brāhmana caste and the Brāhmana quality are two distinct things.

As there are *sattva, rajas* and *tamas*—one or other of these gunas more or less—in every man, so the qualities which make a Brāhmana, Kshatriya, Vaishya or a Shudra are inherent in every man, more or less. But at time one or other of these qualities predominates in him in varying degrees and is manifested accordingly. Take a man in his different pursuits, for example: when he is engaged in serving another for pay, he is in Shudra-hood; when he is busy transacting some piece of business for profit, on his account, he is a Vaishya; when he fights to right wrongs then the qualities of a Kshatriya come out in him; and when he meditates on God, or passes his time in conversation about Him, then he is a Brāhmana. Naturally, it is quite possible for one to be changed from one caste into another. Otherwise, how did Viswamitra become a Brāhmana and Parashurama a Kshatriya?

The means of European civilization is the sword; of the Aryans, the division into different *varnas* is the stepping-stone to civilization, making one rise higher and higher in proportion to one's learning and culture. In Europe, it is everywhere victory to the strong and death to the weak. In the land of Bharata, every social rule is for the protection of the weak.

Such is our ideal of caste, as meant for raising all humanity slowly and gently towards the realization of that great ideal of spiritual man, who is non-resisting, calm, steady, worshipful, pure and meditative. In that ideal there is God.

We believe in Indian caste as one of the greatest social institutions that the Lord gave to man. We also believe that though the unavoidable defects, foreign persecutions, and above all, the monumental ignorance and pride of many Brāhmanas who do not deserve the name, have thwarted in many ways, the legitimate fructification of this most glorious Indian institution, it has already worked wonders for the land of Bharata and is destined to lead Indian humanity to its goal.

Caste should not go; but should only be readjusted occasionally. Within the old structure is to be found life enough for the building of two hundred thousand new ones. It is sheer nonsense to desire the abolition of caste.

Inequality of Privilege Vitiates the System

It is in the nature of society to form itself into groups; and what will go will be these privileges! Caste is a natural order. I can perform one duty in social life, and you another; you can govern a country, and I can mend a pair of old shoes, but that is no reason why you are greater than I, for can you mend my shoes? Can I govern the country? I am clever in mending shoes, you are clever in reading Vedas, that is no reason why you should trample on my head; why if one commits murder should he be praised and if another steals an apple why should he be hanged? This will have to go.

Caste is good. That is the only natural way of solving life. Men must form themselves into groups, and you cannot get rid of that. Wherever you go there will be caste. But that does not mean that there should be these privileges. They should be knocked on the head. If you teach Vedanta to the fisherman, he will say, "I am as good a man as you, I am a fisherman, you are a philosopher, but I have the same God in me, as you have in you." And that is what we want, no privilege for anyone, equal chances for all; let everyone be taught that the Divine is within, and everyone will work out his own salvation. The days of exclusive privileges and exclusive claims are gone, gone for ever from the soil of India.

Untouchability—a Superstitious Accretion

Formerly the characteristic of the noble-minded was —(*tribhuvanamupakāra shrenibhih priyamānah*) "to please the whole universe by one's numerous acts of service", but now it is—I am pure and the whole world is impure. "Don't touch me!" "Don't touch me!" The whole world is impure, and I alone am pure! Lucid *Brahmajnāna*! Bravo! Great God! Nowadays, Brahman is neither in the recesses of the heart, nor in the highest heaven, nor in all beings—now He is in the cooking pot!

We are orthodox Hindus, but we refuse entirely to identify ourselves with "Don't-touchism". That is not Hinduism; it is in none of our books; it is an orthodox superstition, which has interfered with national efficiency all along the line. Religion has entered in the cooking pot. The present religion of the Hindus is neither the path of Knowledge nor that of Reason—it is "Don't-touchism".—"Don't touch me", "Don't touch me"—that exhausts its description.

"Don't-touchism" is a form of mental disease. Beware! All expansion is life, all contraction is death. All love is expansion, all selfishness is contraction. Love is therefore the only law of life. See that you do not lose your lives in this dire irreligion of "Don't-touchism". Must the teaching (*Âtmavat sarvabhuteshu*)—"Looking upon all beings as your own self"—be confined to books alone? How will they grant salvation who cannot feed a hungry mouth with a crumb of bread? How will those, who become impure at the mere breath of others, purify others?

We must cease to tyrannize. To what a ludicrous state are we brought! If a *bhangi* comes to anybody as a *bhangi*, he would be shunned as the plague; but no sooner does he get a cupful of water poured upon his head with some mutterings of prayers by a *pādri*, and get a coat to his back, no matter how threadbare, and come into the room of the most orthodox Hindu, I don't see the man who then dare refuse him a chair and a hearty shake of hands! Irony can go no farther.

Just see, for want of sympathy from the Hindus thousands of *pariahs* in Madras are turning Christians. Don't think that this is simply due to the pinch of hunger; it is because they do not get any sympathy from us. We are day and night calling out to them "Don't touch us! Don't touch us!" Is there any compassion or kindliness of heart in the country? Only a class of "Don't-touchists"; kick such customs out! I sometimes feel the urge to break the barriers of "Don't-touchism", go at once and call out, "Come all who are poor, miserable, wretched and downtrodden", and to bring them all together. Unless they rise, the Mother will not awake.

Each Hindu, I say, is a brother to every other, and it is we, who have degraded them by our outcry, "Don't touch", "Don't touch"! And so the whole country has been plunged to the utmost depths of meanness, cowardice and ignorance. These men have to be lifted; words of hope and faith have to be proclaimed to them. We have to tell them, "You are also men like us and you have all the rights that we have."

Solution of the Caste Problem

Our solution of the caste question is not degrading those who are already high up, is not running amuck through food and drink, is not jumping out of our own limits in order to have more enjoyment, but it comes by every one of us fulfilling the dictates of our Vedantic religion, by our attaining spirituality and by our becoming the ideal Brāhmana. There is a law laid on each one of you in this land by your ancestors, whether you are Aryans, or non-Aryans, *rishis* or Brāhmanas or the very lowest outcastes. The command is the same to you all, that you must make progress without stopping, and that from the highest man to the lowest *pariah*, every one in this country has to try and become the ideal Brāhmana. This Vedantic idea is applicable not only here but over the whole world.

The Brāhmana-hood is the ideal of humanity in India as wonderfully put forward by Shankaracharya at the beginning of his commentary on the *Gitā*, where he speaks about the reason for Krishna's coming as a preacher for the preservation of Brāhmana-hood, of Brāhmana-ness. That was the great end. This Brāhmana, the man of God, he who has known Brahman, the ideal man, the perfect man, must remain; he must not go. And with all the defects of the caste now we know that we must all be ready to give to the Brāhmanas this credit, that from them have come more men with real Brāhmana-ness in them than from all the other castes. That is true. That is the credit due to them from all the other castes. We must be bold enough, must be brave enough to speak their defects, but at the same time we must give the credit that is due to them.

Therefore, it is no use fighting among the castes. What good will it do? It will divide us all the more, weaken us all the more, degrade us all the more. The solution is not by bringing down the higher, but by raising the lower up to the level of the higher. And that is the line of work that is found in all our books, in spite of what you may hear from some people whose knowledge of their own Scriptures and whose capacity to understand the mighty plans of the ancients are only zero. What is the plan? The ideal at one end is the Brāhmana and the ideal at the other end is the *chandāla*, and the whole work is to raise the *chandāla* up to the Brāhmana. Slowly and slowly you find more and more privileges granted to them.

I regret that in modern times there should be so much discussion between the castes. This must stop. It is useless on both sides, especially on the side of the higher caste, the Brāhmana, because, the day for these privileges and exclusive claims is gone. The duty of every aristocracy is to dig its own grave, and the sooner it does so, the better. The more he delays, the more it will fester and the worse death it will die. It is the duty of the Brāhmana, therefore, to work for the salvation of the rest of mankind, in India. If he does that and so long as he does that, he is a Brāhmana.

Any one who claims to be a Brāhmana, then, should prove his pretensions, first by manifesting that spirituality, and next by raising others to the same status. We earnestly entreat the Brāhmanas not to forget the ideal of India—the production of a universe of Brāhmanas, pure as purity, good as God Himself: this was at the beginning, says the *Mahābhārata* and so will it be in the end.

It seems that most of the modern Brāhmanas are only nursing a false pride of birth; and any schemer, native or foreign, who can pander to this vanity and inherent laziness, by fulsome sophistry, appears to satisfy most.

Beware Brāhmanas, this is the sign of death! Arise and show your manhood, your Brāhmana-hood, by raising the non-Brāhmanas around you—not in the spirit of a master—not with the rotten canker of egotism crawling with superstitions and the charlatanry of East and West—but in the spirit of a servant.

To the Brāhmanas I appeal, that they must work hard to raise the Indian people by teaching them what they know, by giving out the culture that they have accumulated for centuries. It is clearly the duty of the Brāhmanas of India to remember what real Brāhmanahood is. As Manu says, all these privileges and honours are given to the Brāhmana because, "with him is the treasury of virtue". He must open that treasury and distribute its valuables to the world.

It is true that he was the earliest preacher to the Indian races, he was the first to renounce everything in order to attain to the higher realization of life, before others could reach to the idea. It was not his fault that he marched ahead of the other castes. Why did not the other castes so understand and do as they did? Why did they sit down and be lazy, and let the Brāhmanas win the race?

But it is one thing to gain an advantage, and another thing to preserve it for evil use. Whenever power is used for evil it becomes diabolical; it must be used for good only. So this accumulated culture of ages of which the Brāhmana has been the trustee, he must now give to the people at large, and it was because he did not give it to the people, that the Mohammedan invasion was possible. It was because he did not open this treasury to the people from the beginning, that for a thousand years we have been trodden under the heels of everyone who chose to come to India; it was through that we have become degraded, and the first task must be to break open the cells that hide the wonderful treasures which our common ancestors accumulated; bring them out, and give them to everybody, and the Brāhmana must be the first to do it. There is an old superstition in Bengal that if the cobra that bites, sucks out his own poison from the patient, the man must survive. Well then, the Brāhmana must suck out his own poison.

To the non-Brāhmana castes I say, wait, be not in a hurry. Do not seize every opportunity of fighting the

Brāhmana, because as I have shown, you are suffering from your own fault. Who told you to neglect spirituality and Sanskrit learning? What have you been doing all this time? Why have you been indifferent? Why do you now fret and fume because somebody else had more brains, more energy, more pluck and go than you? Instead of wasting your energies in vain discussions and quarrels in the newspapers, instead of fighting and quarrelling in your own homes—which is sinful—use all your energies in acquiring the culture which the Brāhmana has, and the thing is done. Why do you not become Sanskrit scholars? Why do you not spend millions to bring Sanskrit education to all the castes of India? That is the question. The moment you do these things, you are equal to the Brāhmana! That is the secret of power in India.

The only safety, I tell you men who belong to the lower castes, the only way to raise your condition is to study Sanskrit, and this fighting and writing and frothing against the higher castes is in vain, it does no good, and it creates fight and quarrel, and this race, unfortunately already divided, is going to be divided more and more. The only way to bring about the levelling of castes is to appropriate the culture, the education which is the strength of the higher castes.

CHAPTER VII

UPLIFT OF WOMEN

Hindu Women's Ideal

Sita is the very type of the true Indian woman, for, all the Indian ideals of a perfected woman have grown out of that one life of Sita; and here she stands these thousands of years, commanding the worship of every man, woman, and child, through the length and breadth of the land of Aryāvarta. There she will always be, this glorious Sita, purer than purity itself, all patience and all suffering. She who suffered that life of suffering without a murmur, she the ever-chaste and ever-pure wife, she the ideal of the people, the ideal of the gods, the great Sita, our national God she must always remain. All our mythology may vanish, even our Vedas may depart, and our Sanskrit language may vanish for ever, but so long as there will be five Hindus living here, even if only speaking the most vulgar *patois*, there will be the story of Sita present, mark my words. Sita has gone into the very vitals of our race. She is there in the blood of every Hindu man and woman; we are all children of Sita.

How different is the ideal in India from that of the West! The West says, "Do. Show your power by doing." India says, "Show your power by suffering." The West has solved the problem of how much a man can have. India has solved the problem of how little a man can have. The two extremes, you see. Sita is typical of India —the idealized India. The question is not whether she ever lived, whether the story is history or not, we know that the ideal is there. There is no other *pauranic* story that has so permeated the whole nation, so entered into its very life, and has so tingled in every drop of blood of the race, as this ideal of Sita.

Sita was chastity itself, she would never touch the body of another man except that of her husband. Sita is the name in India for everything that is good, pure and holy; everything that in woman we call womanly. If a priest has to bless a woman, he says, "Be Sita!" If he blesses a child, he says, "Be Sita!" They are all children of Sita, and are struggling to be Sita, the patient, the all-suffering, the ever-faithful, the ever-pure wife. Through all the suffering she experiences there is not one harsh word against Rama. She takes it as her own duty and performs her own part in it. Think of the terrible injustice of her being exiled to the forest! But Sita knows no bitterness. That is, again, the Indian ideal. Sita was a true Indian by nature; she never returned injury.

I know that the race that produced Sita—even if it only dreamt of her—has a reverence for woman that is unmatched on the earth. There is many a burden bound with legal tightness on the shoulders of Western woman that is utterly unknown to ours. We have our wrongs and our exceptions certainly, but so have they. We must never forget that all over the globe the general effort is to express love and tenderness and uprightness, and that national customs are only the nearest vehicles of this expression. With regard to the domestic virtues I have no hesitation in saying that our Indian methods have in many ways advantage over all others.

Still on this sacred soil of India, this land of Sita and Savitri, among women may be found such character, such spirit of service, such affection, compassion, contentment and reverence, as I could not find anywhere else in the world! In the West, the women did not very often seem to me to be women at all, they appeared to be quite the replicas of men! Driving vehicles, drudging in offices, attending schools, doing professional duties! In India alone the sight of feminine modesty and reserve soothes the eye!

Any attempt to modernise our women, if it tries to take our women away from that ideal of Sita, is immediately a failure, as we see every day. The women of India must grow and develop in the footprints of Sita, and that is the only way.

Their Social Status: Ancient and Modern

We should not allow the sudden influx of European criticism, and our consequent sense of contrast, to make us acquiesce too readily in the notion of the inequality of our women. Circumstances have forced upon us, for many centuries, the woman's need of protection. This and not her inferiority, is the true reading of our customs. Could anything be more complete than the equality of boys and girls in our old forest universities? Read our Sanskrit dramas—read the story of Shakuntala, and see if Tennyson's 'Princess' has anything to teach us!

In Malabar the women lead in everything. Exceptional

cleanliness is apparent everywhere and there is the greatest impetus to learning. When I myself was in that country, I met many women who spoke good Sanskrit, while in the rest of India not one woman in a million can speak it. Mastery elevates and servitude debases. Malabar has never been conquered either by the Portuguese, or by the Mussalmans. The Dravidians were a non-Aryan race of Central Asia, who preceded the Aryans, and those of Southern India were the most civilized. Women with them stood higher than men.

The Aryan and Semitic ideals of woman have always been diametrically opposed. Amongst the Semites the presence of woman is considered dangerous to devotion, and she may not perform any religious function, even such as the killing of a bird for food: according to the Aryan a man cannot perform a religious action without a wife.

In the highest truth of the Parabrahman, there is no distinction of sex. We only notice this in the relative plane. And the more the mind becomes introspective, the more that idea of difference vanishes. Ultimately when the mind is wholly merged in the homogeneous and undifferentiated Brahman then such ideas as this is a man or that a woman do not remain at all. We have actually seen this in the life of Sri Ramakrishna. Therefore do I say that though outwardly there may be difference between men and women, in their real nature there is none. Therefore if a man can be a knower of Brahman, why cannot a woman attain to the same knowledge?

In what scriptures do you find statements that women

are not competent for knowledge and devotion? In the period of degradation, when the priests made the other castes incompetent to the study of the Vedas, they deprived the women also of all their rights. Modern Hinduism is largely Paurānika, that is, post-Buddhistic in origin. Dayananda Saraswati pointed out that though a wife is absolutely necessary in the Sacrifice of the domestic fire, which is a Vedic rite, she may not touch the *shālagrāma shilā,* or the household-idol, because that dates from the later period of the *Purānas.* Otherwise you will find that in the Vedic or Upanishadic age Maitreyi, Gargi, and other ladies of revered memory have taken the places of *rishis* through their skill in discussing about Brahman. In an assembly of a thousand Brāhmanas who were all erudite in the Vedas, Gargi boldly challenged Yājnavalkya in a discussion about Brahman.

Their Uplift: a Crying Need

When such ideal women were entitled to spiritual knowledge, then why shall not the women have the same privilege now? What has happened once can certainly happen again. History repeats itself.

You always criticise the women, but say, what have you done for their uplift? Writing down *smritis* etc., and binding them by hard rules, the men have turned the women into mere manufacturing machines! They have all the time been trained in helplessness, servile dependence on others, and so they are good only to weep their eyes out at the slightest approach of a mishap or danger.

All nations have attained greatness, by paying proper respect to the women. That country and that nation which do not respect the women have never become great, nor will ever be in future. The principal reason why your race has so much degenerated is that you had no respect for these living images of *Shakti*. Manu says, "Where women are respected there the gods delight; and where they are not, there all works and efforts come to naught." (*Manu-samhitā* III. 56). There is no hope of rise for that family or country where there is no estimation of women, where they live in sadness.

Do you know who is the real '*Shakti*-worshipper'? It is he who knows that God is the Omnipresent Force in the universe, and sees in women the manifestation of that Force. Can you better the condition of your women? Then there will be hope for your well-being. Otherwise you remain as backward as you are now. The uplift of the women, the awakening of the masses, must come first, and then only can any real good come about for the country, for India. If the women are raised, then their children will by their noble actions glorify the name of the country—then will culture, knowledge, power and devotion awaken in the country.

How to Tackle Their Problems

It is wrong, a thousand times wrong, if any of you dare to say, "I will work out the salvation of this woman or child." I am asked again and again, what I think of the widow problem and what I think of the woman question. Let me answer once for all—am I a widow that you ask me that nonsense? Am I a woman that you ask me that question again and again? Who are you to solve women's problems? Are you the Lord God that you should rule over every widow and every woman? Hands off! They will solve their own problems.

In my opinion society in every country shapes itself out of its own initiative. So we need not trouble our heads prematurely about such reforms as the abolition of early marriage, the remarriage of widows and so on. Our part of the duty lies in imparting true education to all men and women in society. As an outcome of that education they will of themselves be able to know what is good for them and what is bad, and will spontaneously eschew the latter. It will not be then necessary to pull down or set up anything in society by coercion. Our right of interference is limited entirely to giving education. Women must be put in a position to solve their own problems in their own way. No one can or ought to do this for them. And our Indian women are as capable of doing it as any in the world.

Education They Require for Solving Their Problems

With such materials of great promise, you could not, alas, work out their uplift! You did not try to infuse the light of knowledge into them! For if they get the right sort of education, they may well turn out to be the ideal women in the world. Of course, they have many and grave problems, but none that are not to be solved by that magic word 'education'.

To make a beginning in women's education: our Hindu women easily understand what chastity means, because it is their heritage. Now, first of all, intensify that ideal within them above everything else, so that they may develop a strong character by the force of which, in every stage of their lives, whether married, or single if they prefer to remain so, they will not be in the least afraid even to give up their lives rather than flinch an inch from their chastity. Is it little heroism to be able to sacrifice one's life for the sake of one's ideal, whatever that ideal may be?

History and the *Purānas*, religion, arts, science, house-keeping, cooking, sewing, hygiene—the simple essential points in these subjects ought to be taught to our women. It is not good to let them touch novels and fiction. But only teaching rites of worship won't do; their education must be an eye-opener in all matters. Ideal characters must always be presented before the view of the girls to imbue them with a devotion to lofty principles of selflessness. The noble examples of Sita, Savitri, Damayanti, Lilavati, Khana and Mira should be brought home to their minds and they should be inspired to mould their own lives in the light of these. Along with other things they should acquire the spirit of valour and heroism. In the present day it has become necessary for them also to learn self-defence. See how grand was the Queen of Jhansi! With such an education women will solve their own problems.

We must see to their growing up as ideal matrons of home in time. The children of such mothers will make further progress in the virtues that distinguish the mothers. It is only in the homes of educated and pious mothers that great men are born.

Studying the present needs of the age, it seems imperative to train some of them up in the ideals of renunciation, so that they will take up the vow of lifelong virginity, fired with the strength of that virtue of chastity which is innate in their life-blood, from hoary antiquity. Along with that they should be taught sciences and other things which would be of benefit, not only to them but to others as well, and knowing this they would easily learn these things and feel pleasure in doing so. Our motherland requires for her well-being some of her children to become such pure-souled *brahmachārinis.*

By their example and through their endeavours to hold the national ideal before the eyes of the people, a revolution in thoughts and aspirations will take place. How do matters stand now? Somehow, the parents must dispose of a girl in marriage, if she be nine or ten years of age! And what a rejoicing of the whole family if a child is born to her at the age of thirteen! If the trend of such ideas is reversed, then there is some hope for the ancient *shraddhā* to return. And what to talk of those who will practise *brahmacharya*—think how much *shraddhā* and faith in themselves will be theirs! And what a power for good will they be!

So shall we bring to the need of India great fearless women—women worthy to continue the traditions of Sanghamitta, Lila, Ahalya Bai, and Mira Bai—women fit to be mothers of heroes, because they are pure and selfless, strong with the strength that comes of touching the feet of God.

The Swami's Plan

Women are the living embodiment of the Divine

Mother, whose external manifestations appealing to the senses have maddened men, but whose internal manifestations such as knowledge, devotion, discrimination and dispassion make man omniscient, of unfailing purpose, and a knower of Brahman. "She when pleased becomes propitious and the cause of the freedom of man." (*Chandi*). Without propitiating the Mother by worship and obeisance not even Brahmā and Vishnu have the power to elude Her grasp and attain to freedom. Therefore for the worship of these family goddesses, in order to manifest the Brahman within them, I shall establish the women's *Math*.

There shall be a girls' school attached to this *Math*, in which religious scriptures, literature, Sanskrit, grammar, and even some amount of English should be taught. Other matters such as sewing, culinary art, rules of domestic work, and upbringing of children will also be taught, while *japa*, worship and meditation, etc., shall form an indispensable part of the teaching. The duty of teaching in the school ought to devolve in every respect on educated widows and *brahmachārinis*. It is good to avoid in this country any association of men with women's schools. The elder *brahmachārinis* will take charge of the training of the girl students in *brahmacharya*.

After five or six years' training in this *Math*, the guardians of the girls may marry them. If deemed fit for *yoga* and religious life, with the permission of their guardians they will be allowed to stay in this *Math*, taking the vow of celibacy. These celibate nuns will in time be the teachers and preachers of the *Math*. In villages and towns they will open centres and strive for the spread of female education. Through such devout preachers of character there will be the real spread of female education in this country.

So long as the students will remain associated with this *Math*, they must observe *brahmacharya* as the basic idea of this *Math*. Spirituality, sacrifice and self-control will be the motto of the pupils of this *Math*, and service or *seva-dharma* the vow of their life. In view of such ideal lives, who will not respect and have faith in them? If the life of the women of this country be moulded in such fashion, then only will there be the reappearance of such ideal characters as Sita, Savitri, and Gargi.

6

CHAPTER VIII

INVIGORATING CULTURAL LIFE

Preservation of Cultural Integrity

We must grow according to our nature. Vain is to attempt the lines of action that foreign societies have engrafted upon us; it is impossible. Glory unto God, that it is impossible, that we cannot be twisted and tortured into the shape of other nations. I do not condemn the institutions of other races; they are good for them, but not for us. With other sciences, other institutions, and other traditions behind them, they have got their present system. We, with our traditions, with thousands of years of *karma* behind us, naturally can only follow our own bent, run in our own grooves and that we shall have to do.

We cannot become Westerns, therefore imitating the Western is useless. Suppose you can imitate the Westerns, that moment you will die, you will have no more life in you. A stream is taking its rise, away beyond where time began, flowing through millions of ages of human history; do you mean to get hold of that stream, and push it back to its source, to a Himalayan glacier? Even if that were practicable it would not be possible for you to be Europeanised. If you find it is impossible for the European to throw off the few centuries of old culture which there is in the West, do you think it is possible for you to throw off the culture of shining scores of centuries? It cannot be. To Europeanise India is therefore an impossible and foolish task.

There are two great obstacles on our path in India, the Scylla of old orthodoxy, and the Charybdis of modern European civilization. Of these two, I vote for the old orthodoxy, and not for the Europeanised system; for the old orthodox man may be ignorant, he may be crude but he is a man, he has a faith, he has strength, he stands on his own feet; while the Europeanised man has no backbone, he is a mass of heterogeneous ideas picked up at random from every source—and these ideas are unassimilated, undigested, unharmonised. He does not stand on his own feet, and his head is turning round and round. Where is the motive power of his work? In a few patronising pats from the English people. His schemes of reforms, his vehement vituperations against the evils of certain social customs have, as the mainspring, some European patronage. Why are some of our customs called evils? Because the Europeans say so. That is about the reason he gives. I would not submit to that. Stand and die in your strength; if there is any sin in the world, it is weakness; avoid all weakness, for weakness is sin, weakness is death. These unbalanced creatures are not yet formed into distinct personalities; what are we to call them—men, women, or animals? While those old orthodox people were staunch and were men.

Therefore, between these two, the case of the orthodox man who has the whole of that life-spring of the race, spirituality, and the other man whose hands are full of Western imitation-jewels but who has no hold on the life-giving principle, spirituality—of these, I do not doubt that everyone will agree that we should choose the first, the orthodox, because there is some hope in him. He has the national theme, something to hold to, so he will live, but the other will die. If you give up that spirituality and go after the materializing civilization of the West, the result will be that in three generations you will be an extinct race; because the backbone of the nation will be broken, the foundation upon which the national edifice has been built will be undermined, and the result will be annihilation all round.

If any one preaches in India the ideal of eating and drinking and making merry, if anyone wants to apotheosise the material world into a God, that man is a liar; he has no place in this holy land, the Indian mind does not want to listen to him. Aye, in spite of the sparkle and glitter of Western civilization, in spite of all its polish and its marvellous manifestation of power, I tell them to their face, that it is all vain. It is vanity of vanities. God alone lives. The soul alone lives. Spirituality alone lives. Hold on to that.

Broadening of Cultural Outlook

We cannot do without the world outside India; it was our foolishness that we thought we could, and we have paid the penalty by about a thousand years of slavery. We have paid the penalty; let us do it no more. All such foolish ideas that Indians must not go out of India, are childish. They must be knocked on the head; the more you go out and travel among the nations of the world, the better for you and your country. If you had done that for hundreds of years past you would not be here today at the feet of every nation that wants to rule India. The first manifest effect of life is expansion. You must expand if you want to live. The moment you have ceased to expand, death is upon you, danger is ahead.

Several dangers are in the way, and one is that of the extreme conception that we are the people in the world. With all my love for India and with all my patriotism and veneration for the ancients, I cannot but think that we have to learn many things from other nations. We must be always ready to sit at the feet of all, for, mark you, everyone can teach us great lessons. Says our great lawgiver, Manu: "Receive some good knowledge even from the low-born and from the man of lowest birth, learn by service the road to heaven." We, therefore, as true children of Manu, must obey his commands, and be ready to learn the lessons of this life, or the life hereafter from anyone who can teach us.

It is Greece that speaks through everything in Europe. Every building, every piece of furniture has the impress of Greece upon it; European science and art are nothing but Grecian. Today the ancient Greece is meeting the ancient Hindu on the soil of India. Thus, slowly and silently the leaven has come, the broadening out, the life-giving, and the revivalist movement, that we see all around us, has been worked out by these forces together. A broader and more generous conception of life is before us, and although at first we have been deluded a little and wanted to narrow things down, we are finding out today that these generous impulses which are at work, these broader conceptions of life, are the logical interpretation of what is in our ancient books. They are the carrying out to the rigorously logical effect of the primary conceptions of our own ancestors. To become broad, to go out, to amalgamate, to universalize, is the end of our aims.

We have many things to learn from the West. We should learn from the West her arts and sciences. We have to gain a little in material knowledge, in the power of organization, in the ability to handle powers, organizing powers, in bringing the best results out of the smallest of causes. This perhaps to a certain extent we may learn from the West.

We must travel, we must go to foreign parts. We must see how the engine of society works in other countries, and keep free and open communication with what is going on in the minds of other nations, if we really want to be a nation again. Stand on your own feet, and assimilate what you can; learn from every nation, take what is of use to you.

But remember that as Hindus everything else must be subordinated to our own national ideals. The secret of a true Hindu's character lies in the subordination of his knowledge of European science and learning, of his wealth, position and name, to that one principal theme which is inborn in every Hindu child—the spirituality and purity of the race.

Two Viewpoints: Eastern and Western

The voice of Asia has been the voice of religion. The voice of Europe is the voice of politics. Each is great in its own sphere. The voice of Europe is the voice of ancient Greece. To the Greek mind, his immediate society was all in all. Beyond that it is Barbarian—none but the Greek has the right to live. Whatever the Greeks do is right and correct; whatever else there exists in the world is neither right nor correct, nor should be allowed to live. It is intensely human in its sympathies, intensely natural, intensely artistic, therefore. The Greek lives entirely in this world. He does not care to dream. Even his poetry is practical. His gods and goddesses are not only human beings, but intensely human with all human passions and feelings almost the same as with any of us. He loves what is beautiful, but, mind you, it is always external nature; the beauty of the hills, of the snows, of the flowers; the beauty of forms and of figures; the beauty in the human face, and, more often, in the human form—that is what the Greeks like. And the Greeks being the teachers of all subsequent Europeanism, the voice of Europe is Greek.

There is another type in Asia. The Oriental love of the beautiful and of the sublime developed itself in another direction. It looked inside and not outside. There is also the thirst for Nature; and there is also the same thirst for power; there is also the same thirst for excellence, the same idea of the Greek and Barbarian; but it has extended over a huge circle. In Asia, even today, birth or colour or language never makes a race. That which makes a race is its religion. No matter if a Buddhist is a Chinaman, or is a man from Persia, they think that they are brothers, because of their professing the same religion. Religion is the tie, the unity of humanity. And then again, the Oriental, for the same reason, is a visionary, is a born dreamer. The ripples of the waterfalls, the songs of the birds, the beauties of the sun and moon and the stars and the whole earth, are pleasant enough; but they are not sufficient for the Oriental mind. He wants to dream a dream beyond. He wants to go beyond the present. The present, as it were, is nothing to him.

The Orient has been the cradle of human race for ages, and all the vicissitudes of fortune are there. Kingdoms succeeding kingdoms; empires succeeding empires; human power, glory and wealth, all rolling down there: a Golgotha of power, and learning. That is the Orient: a Golgotha of power, of kingdoms, of learning. No wonder, the Oriental mind looks with contempt upon the things of this world and naturally wants to see something that changeth not, something which dieth not, something which in the midst of this world of misery and death is eternal, blissful, undying. An Oriental Prophet never tires of insisting upon these ideals; and, as for Prophets, you may also remember that without one exception all the Messengers were Orientals.

If those whose eyes have been blinded by the glamour of material things, whose whole dedication of life is to eating and drinking and enjoying, whose ideal of possession is lands and gold, whose ideal of pleasure is that of the senses, whose God is money, and whose goal is a life of ease and comfort in this world and death after that, whose minds never look forward, and who rarely think of anything higher than the sense objects in the midst of which they live: if such as these go to India, what do they see? Poverty, squalor, superstition, darkness, hideousness everywhere. Why? Because in their minds enlightenment means dress, education, social politeness. Whereas Occidental nations have used every effort to improve their material position, India has done differently.

There live the only men in the world, who, in the whole history of humanity, never went beyond their frontiers to conquer anyone, who never coveted that which belonged to anyone else, whose only fault was that their lands were so fertile, and they accumulated wealth by the hard labour of their hands, and so tempted other nations to come and despoil them. They are contented to be despoiled, and to be called Barbarians, and in return, they want to send to this world, visions of the Supreme, to lay bare for the world the secrets of human nature, to rend the veil that conceals the real man, because they know the dream, because they know that behind this materialism lives the real, divine nature of man which no sin can tarnish, no crime can spoil, no lust can taint; which fire cannot burn, nor water wet, which heat cannot dry, nor death kill; and to them this true nature of man is as real as is any material object to the senses of an Occidental.

There it is, that when a man declares that this is a world of ideas, that it is all a dream, he casts off clothes and property to demonstrate that what he believes and thinks is true. There it is that a man sits on the bank of a river, when he has known that life is eternal, and wants to give up his body just as nothing, just as you can give up a bit of straw. Therein lies their heroism, that they are ready to face death as a brother because they are convinced that there is no death for them. Therein lies the strength that has made them invincible through hundreds of years of oppression and foreign invasion and tyranny. The nation lives today, and in that nation even in the days of the direct disaster, spiritual giants have never failed to arise. Asia produces giants in spirituality, just as the Occident produces giants in politics, giants in science.

You people of the West are practical in your own department, in military affairs, and in managing political circles and other things. Perhaps, the Oriental is not practical in those ways, but he is practical in his own field: he is practical in religion. Just as you are brave to jump at the mouth of a cannon with a hurrah, just as you are brave in the name of patriotism, to stand up and give up your lives for your country, so are they brave in the name of God. If one preaches a philosophy, tomorrow there are hundreds who will struggle their best to make it practical in their lives. If a man preaches that standing on one foot would lead to salvation, he will immediately get five hundred to stand on one foot. You may call it ludicrous; but, mark you, beneath that is their philosophy—that intense practicality.

In the West, plans of salvation mean intellectual gymnastics, plans which are never worked out, never brought into practical life. In the West, the preacher who talks the best is the greatest preacher. It will take a long time for the Westerners to understand the higher spirituality. Everything is pound, shilling and pence to them. If a religion brings them money or health or beauty, or long life, they will all flock to it, otherwise not. Just as the Western ideal is to keep up luxury in practical life, so ours is to keep up the highest form of spirituality, to demonstrate that religion is not merely frothy words, but can be carried out, every bit of it, in his life.

Liberty is the first condition of growth. Your ancestors gave every liberty to the soul, and religion grew. They put the body under every bondage and society did not grow. The opposite is the case in the West—every liberty to society, none to religion. The West wants every bit of spirituality through social improvement. The East wants every bit of social power through spirituality.

Spiritual knowledge is the only thing that can destroy our miseries for ever; any other knowledge satisfies wants only for a time. It is only with the knowledge of the spirit that the faculty of want is annihilated for ever. Great indeed are the manifestations of muscular power, and marvellous the manifestations of intellect, expressing themselves through machines by the appliances of science; yet, none of these are more potent than the influence which spirit exerts upon the world.

Machines never made mankind happy, and never will make. He who is trying to make us believe this, will claim that happiness is in machine, but it is always in the mind. The man alone who is the lord of his mind can become happy, and none else. And what, after all, is this power of machinery? Why should a man who can send a current of electricity through a wire be called a very great man, and a very intelligent man? Does not Nature do a million times more than that every moment? Why not then fall down and worship Nature? What avails it if you have power over the whole of the world, if you have mastered every atom in the universe? That will not make you happy unless you have the power of happiness in yourself, until you have conquered yourself.

Man is born to conquer Nature, it is true, but the Occidental means by 'Nature', only physical or external Nature. It is true that external Nature is majestic, with its mountains, and oceans, and rivers, and with its infinite powers and varieties. Yet there is a more majestic internal Nature of man, higher than the sun, moon and stars, higher than this earth of ours, higher than the physical universe, transcending these lives of ours; and it affords another field of study. There the Orientals excel, just as the Occidentals excel in the other.

Both Necessary for Human Progress

To the Oriental, the world of spirit is as real, as to the Occidental is the world of senses. In the spiritual, the Oriental finds everything he wants or hopes for; in it he finds all that makes life real to him. To the Occidental he is a dreamer; to the Oriental the Occidental is a dreamer, playing with ephemeral toys and he laughs to think that grown-up men and women should make so much of a handful of matter which they will have to leave sooner or later. Each calls the other a dreamer. But the Oriental ideal is as necessary for the progress of the human race as is the Occidental, and I think it is more necessary.

Therefore, it is fitting that, whenever there is a spiritual adjustment it should come from the Orient. It is also fitting that when the Oriental wants to learn about machine-making, he should sit at the feet of the Occidental and learn from him. When the Occident wants to learn about the Spirit, about God, about the soul, about the meaning and the mystery of this universe, he must sit at the feet of the Orient to learn.

This world of ours is on the plan of the division of labour. It is vain to say that one man shall possess everything. Yet how childish we are! The baby in its ignorance, thinks that its doll is the only possession that is to be coveted in this whole universe. So a nation which is great in the possession of material power, thinks that that is all that is to be coveted, that that is all that is meant by progress, that that is all that is meant by civilization, and if there are other nations which do not care for possession, and do not possess that power, they are not fit to live, their whole existence is useless! On the other hand, another nation may think that mere material civilization is utterly useless. From the Orient came the voice which once told the world that if a man possesses everything that is under the sun and does not possess spirituality, what avails it? This is the Oriental type; the other is the Occidental type. Each of these types has its grandeur, each has its glory. The present adjustment will be the harmonizing, the mingling of these two ideals.

Propagation of Indian Culture

The only condition of national life, of awakened and vigorous national life, is the conquest of the world by Indian thought. Indian thought, philosophical and spiritual, must once more go over and conquer the world. There have been great conquering races in the world.

We also have been great conquerors. The story of our conquest has been described by that noble Emperor of India, Asoka, as the conquest of religion and spirituality. Once more the world must be conquered by India.

They will tell you every day that we had better look to our own homes first, and then go to work outside. But I will tell you in plain language that you work best when you work for others. The best work that you ever did for yourselves was when you worked for others, trying to disseminate your ideas, in foreign languages, beyond the seas.

Let foreigners come and flood the land with their armies, never mind. Up, India, and conquer the world with your spirituality. Aye, as has been declared on this soil first, love must conquer hatred, hatred cannot conquer itself. Materialism and all its miseries can never be conquered by materialism. Armies when they attempt to conquer armies only multiply and make brutes of humanity. Spirituality must conquer the West.

Slowly they are finding out that what they want is spirituality to preserve them as nations. They are waiting for it, they are eager for it. Where is the supply to come from? Where are the men ready to go out to every country in the world with the messages of the great sages of India? Where are the men who are ready to sacrifice everything, so that this message shall reach every corner of the world? Such heroic souls are wanted to help the spread of truth. Such heroic workers are wanted to go abroad and help to disseminate the great truths of the Vedānta.

The world wants it; without it the world will be

destroyed. The whole of the Western world is on a volcano which may burst tomorrow, go to pieces tomorrow. They have searched every corner of the world and have found no respite. They have drunk deep of the cup of pleasure and found its vanity. Now is the time to work so that India's spiritual ideas may penetrate deep into the West.

Therefore we must go out, exchange our spirituality for anything they have to give us; for the marvels of the region of Spirit we will exchange the marvels of the region of matter. We will not be students always, but teachers also. There cannot be friendship without equality, and there cannot be equality when one party is always the teacher and the other party sits always at his feet. You will have to teach as well as to learn, and you have plenty yet to teach to the world for centuries to come.

At the same time you must not forget that what I mean by the conquest of the world by spiritual thought, is the sending out of the life-giving principles, not the hundreds of superstitions that we have been hugging to our breasts for centuries. They have to be weeded out even on this soil, and thrown aside, so that they may die for ever.

By preaching the profound secrets of the Vedānta religion in the Western world, we shall attract the sympathy and regard of these mighty nations, maintaining for ever the position of their teacher in spiritual matters, and they will remain our teachers in all material concerns. The day when, surrendering the spiritual into their hands, our countrymen would sit at the feet of the

West to learn religion, that day indeed the nationality of this fallen nation will be dead and gone for good.

Nothing will come of crying day and night before them, 'Give me this or give me that'. When there will grow a link of sympathy and regard between both nations by this give-and-take intercourse, there will be then no need for these noisy cries. They will do everything of their own accord. I believe that by this cultivation of religion and the wider diffusion of Vedānta, both this country and the West will gain enormously. To me the pursuit of politics is a secondary means in comparison with this. I will lay down my life to carry out this belief practically.